FOR
CHRIST'S SAKE

A reply to the Bishop of Woolwich's
book HONEST TO GOD and a
positive continuation
of the discussion.

by

O. FIELDING CLARKE, M.A., B.D.

REP

THE RELIGIOUS EDUCATION PRESS LTD.
WALLINGTON   SURREY

First Published August 1963
Second Edition, September 1963

Made and Printed in Great Britain by
Charles Birchall & Sons Ltd.,
Liverpool and London

CONTENTS

Cover illustration by courtesy of
AERO FILMS AND AERO PICTORIAL LTD.

AUTHOR'S PREFACE

MAY I suggest that you *start* reading this book at Part II, page 51, if theology is not your line?

Part II tries to say simply what Christianity is about and where I think the shoe really pinches today if you want to be a Christian. By itself Part II makes sense (or I hope it does).

You can then turn back and read Part I which is a chapter by chapter criticism of the Bishop of Woolwich's book *Honest to God*. This naturally is heavier going and more technical, though as simple as I can make it. After all if the bishop had built a bridge instead of writing a book I could hardly be expected to criticize it as a structure without using engineer's language! The thought-world of religion also has its technical terms, but here their use is cut to a minimum.

'Why did you have to write this book?' someone may ask. Because as a parish priest going among ordinary people I found bewilderment and sometimes indignation at Dr. Robinson's book, or at the provocative extracts from it hurled at them in the press or on the 'telly'.

A few words in the parish magazine clearly wouldn't fill the bill. It needed a small book to refute what I regard as

Dr. Robinson's errors and re-state the Faith in outline. Here then it is.

'One sometimes wonders if the whole thing (Christianity) isn't a gigantic hoax,' said one young parishioner—a product of one of our public-schools and a student. 'Why is he a bishop if he says that sort of thing?' was another comment. Indeed the bishop's book, like the present controversy over the 39 Articles, has again raised in many minds the question what after all does the Church of England stand for? Do the clergy and church-goers honestly believe what they say in church?

Most do : of that I am sure. For my own part I haven't come at all easily to my Faith as an orthodox Anglican. I say 'come to,' but of course Faith is a gift of God for which I am humbly thankful. At one time however (and it was *after* reading theology) I had to give up the idea of being a clergyman. It was only after further reading and thought and a spell in Bermondsey that it became possible for me *honestly* to accept the Church's teachings.

I am therefore by nature sympathetic to those who find it hard to believe, but I am also quite sure that one does not help atheists and agnostics by producing a theology so muddled and watered-down that people have to ask what really is the difference between an agnostic humanist and a Christian. The bishop will not like the suggestion contained in this sentence but it has been made to me—yes, and by a university science graduate !

If this little book helps to re-assure some people in the Christian Faith and perhaps win over others I shall feel it has been worth while writing. It has all had to be done in a few weeks in the midst of all one's other work and I am very conscious of its inadequacies.

In conclusion I want to thank both the Bishop of Woolwich and the S.C.M. Press for permission to use quotations from *Honest to God*. I am also very grateful to Principal John Huxtable for contributing his cordial Foreword. Finally a special thank you to Mr. E. P. Smith and the Religious Education Press Ltd. for their speed and efficiency, and to my wife who has all along given such valuable encouragement and criticism.

O. FIELDING CLARKE

Hazelwood Vicarage, Derby.
Whitsuntide, 1963.

FOREWORD

by

Principal John Huxtable, M.A.

We should all be grateful that *Honest to God* has been so widely welcomed, for in it one of the ablest Anglicans of our time has raised for public discussion questions which we are all tempted to avoid.

If 'truth is never worsted in open conflict' Christians have nothing to lose and in fact everything to gain by frank questioning of the content of their Faith and of the forms in which it is expressed. It may be doubted, however, whether the Bishop of Woolwich has always posed his questions in the most illuminating way, whether the arguments he sets forth are uniformly convincing, or whether his meaning at certain crucial points is at all plain.

Dr Robinson would, of course, be the first to desire that such issues as these should be taken up; and I very much hope that what Mr Fielding Clarke has written will stimulate still further discussion.

I hope, too, that the very many who have been more confused than enlightened by *Honest to God* will find here clues by which to make their own way to a surely-based faith. I am sure that they will be helped to frame the right questions more precisely; and this is always the most important step towards solutions.

New College
London. N.W.3.   JOHN HUXTABLE

PART ONE

A critique of *Honest to God* chapter by chapter

1

RELUCTANT REVOLUTION

TO be a Christian means to have accepted Jesus Christ as the Image of the invisible God. Christians therefore are not explorers seeking for an Image of ultimate reality, the ground of all being, or whatever it may be called. For them Christ is the once for all given Image. He has come and we do not look for another.

Yet equally for a Christian there can never be any pride of possession. Indeed if there be we have already lost what we have claimed to possess. For to accept Christ as the Image of God is not to accept the conclusion of an argument. Christ can only be received in faith and faith is itself the gift of God. 'By grace are ye saved through faith and that not of yourselves, it is the gift of God.'[1] Reason indeed has its place; but when argument has done its best, when philosophy and historical research have shot their last bolt, faith lies beyond.

The Catholic tradition has always claimed that God's existence can be proved, but it still remains that faith, which includes complete committal to God in Jesus Christ, is a grace and a gift.

Dr. Robinson tells us (p. 8) that his faith and

[1] Ephesians 2.8.

9

commitment are not in the least in doubt. On p. 128 he says : 'Christianity stands or falls by revelation, by Christ as the disclosure of the final truth not merely about human nature (that we might accept relatively easily) but about all nature and all reality.' Now 'all reality' must presumably include 'ultimate reality,' and as he says (p. 29) 'God is by definition ultimate reality. And one cannot argue whether ultimate reality *exists*.' And again (p. 128) we read 'for unless the *ousia*, the being of things deep down, *is* Love, of the quality disclosed in the life, death and resurrection of Jesus Christ, then the Christian could have little confidence in affirming the ultimate personal character of reality.' On p. 44 we are told 'our concern is in no way to change the Christian doctrine of God but precisely to see that it does not disappear with this outmoded view' (of the world, that is).

Again on p. 27 Dr. Robinson tells us in comparing his background with that of Dr. John Wren-Lewis that he has never really doubted the fundamental truth of the Christian faith. Finally, on p. 71 we have '(Jesus) was the complete expression, the Word, of God. Through him, as through no one else, God spoke and God acted : when one met him one was met—and saved and judged—by God. And it was to this conviction that the Apostles bore their witness. In this man, in his life, death and resurrection they had experienced God at work; and in the language of their day they confessed, like the centurion at the Cross, "Truly this man was the Son of God."[1] Here was more than just a man : here was a window into God at work. For "God was in Christ reconciling the world to himself".'[2]

All this is unimpeachable orthodoxy, what we should ex-

[1]Mark *15*.39.
[2]II Cor. *5*.19.

pect from the author of that pellucid work *On being the Church in the World*. When some of his fellow bishops say that Dr. Robinson is not a heretic they no doubt have such passages in mind.

But in fact there are really two Dr. Robinsons. The bulk of *Honest to God* has been written by a second Dr. Robinson who is probably heretical and usually (unlike the orthodox Dr. Robinson) muddled.

It is perhaps well that the Preface opens with the words 'It belongs to the office of a bishop in the Church to be a guardian and defender of its doctrine,' and a few lines further on that 'it is going to become increasingly difficult to know what the true defence of Christian truth requires.' Much of the book is based on the old maxim that 'the surest defence is attack,' only this is given a novel interpretation. You attack what you are committed to defend.

Why? Because, as everyone knows, Christianity is losing out in the modern world. This is not a peculiarly British phenomenon. A few years ago Mr. Serge Bolshakoff in a valuable article in the *Church Times* gave a report of his visits to many parts of Europe, both Catholic and Protestant. The picture was roughly the same as it is in Britain, sometimes better, sometimes worse, but on balance much the same.

But it is not with the gulf between Christians and pagans that *Honest to God* is concerned. Rather is it with the alienation of one very important sector of society, the intelligent. It is claimed that some of these at any rate have rejected not the Gospel, but a particular way of thinking about the world. Dr. Robinson finds the antagonism of these people towards what they think the Gospel to be is also to be found in himself, and that he more and more tends to side with them. The frame or mould of religion in which the Faith is normally presented is to be radically criticized, but he seems 'fairly sure' that in retrospect what he has to say will be seen to have erred in not being nearly radical enough.

The first chapter is headed *Reluctant Revolution*. We are reminded that the framework of a three-decker universe —a flat earth with heaven on a vast arch above and hell beneath—has long since been abandoned without any damage to the Faith. Christianity in all its forms has detached itself from pre-Copernican cosmology. For God 'up there' has therefore been substituted God 'out there.' Now this in its turn has to go. In its crude literal form it has been made untenable by such things as the exploit of Major Gagarin !

But it is not clear why 'the idea of a God spiritually or metaphysically "out there" ' also has to go. Dr. Robinson admits that it 'dies very much harder' than the crude idea of God locally in space and that it moulds the imagery employed not only by the classics of the Christian faith but by its most successful modern communicators, such as Dorothy Sayers, C. S. Lewis and J. B. Phillips.

Nevertheless 'we may have to pass through a century or more of re-appraisal before this language ceases to be an offence to faith for a great many people.'[1] There is even a hint that Freud is perhaps right and that God 'out there,' even in the most refined form, is a mere projection and we may have to do without it. 'That is not an attractive proposition.' It is certain to be misunderstood and regarded as a betrayal of what the Bible says by 90 per cent of Church people, and even a 'large percentage' of Dr. Robinson finds this revolution unacceptable—yet he can do no other. Must this happen? What can we put in to replace what is destroyed?

[1] *Honest to God*, p. 15 (Subsequently referred to as H.T.G.).

Here as elsewhere the author is honest enough to admit that he has a split mind. But what is the justification for a bishop, by his office a guardian of the Faith, airing his indecisions in public? He is no longer a Cambridge don for whom endless questioning and probing may be a true vocation. If his doubts are so pressing then he should keep silence till *at least* he can state his views (heretical or not) clearly. One of the absolutely inexcusable features of his book is its incoherence. On page 21 Dr. Robinson admits that he is 'thinking aloud,' 'struggling to think other people's thoughts after them' and unable to 'claim to have understood all I am trying to transmit.' That in a bishop and in a theologian who can write brilliantly appears to many thinking people the height of irresponsibility.

After admitting that he is in a fog he proceeds to point to the three books which have set him thinking along these lines : Paul Tillich's *The Shaking of the Foundations,* Dietrich Bonhoeffer's *Letters and Papers from Prison,* and Rudolf Bultmann's *New Testament and Mythology*—three theologians about whose meaning, as Dr. Wand aptly remarked, the experts disagree wildly. Thank God for stimulating and exciting thinkers !

But if the pastor himself cannot digest the fare provided what chance has the flock of obtaining nourishment? Dr. Robinson admits that the thinking of Tillich, Bonhoeffer and Bultmann 'is still nowhere near being assimilated or digested by the ordinary man in the pew, *nor by most of those who preach and write for him.*'[1] Indeed of himself, even, he says that the full extent of this reluctant revolution is something which 'I have hardly begun to comprehend,' and that he is 'well aware that much of what I shall seek to say will be seriously misunderstood, and *will doubtless de-*

[1] H.T.G. p. 26. *Italics mine.*

serve to be.[1] Exactly. But one cannot have one's cake and eat it. Either one is 'an ordinary churchman' and not 'a professional theologian' or one is a bishop and pastor, in this case with more than ordinary attainments as a theologian. If one is the latter it is one's duty to think *before* speaking and, if one cannot make up one's mind, at least to refrain from expressing the confusion of one's thought in a five shilling paper-back for our means of mass communication to din into the ears of the unfortunate half-educated—the last people on earth to be helped by such incoherence.

Dr. Robinson refers to the Bishop of Middleton's book *Church and People in an Industrial City* (Lutterworth Press) as an example of how Bonhoeffer's views have been taken up by one who has had unique experience of presenting Christianity relevantly on the shop floor, an instance of their beneficent influence in the front line, so to speak. This reference so far from lending him support does exactly the opposite. Anyone who will read pages 232-8 of Edward Wickham's splendid survey of religion in Sheffield referred to by Dr. Robinson will at once be struck by the world of difference between what happens when one has really digested Bonhoeffer, Bultmann and Tillich, and when one merely regurgitates them.

[1]H.T.G. p. 27. *Italics mine.*

2

THE END OF THEISM? AND THE GROUND OF OUR BEING

I AM not a student of Tillich and I do not intend to be drawn into a discussion of the merits (or otherwise) of his system. We are concerned here not with Tillich but what Dr. Robinson has made of him—so far, of course, as this is clear. (Incidentally is it really necessary for a bishop to be flippant about sacred things, in order to convince his readers that in spite of such an obviously 'U' background one is still a human being? God 'like a rich aunt in Australia,' God 'dressed up like Father Christmas,' God 'taking a space trip' etc?).

Basing himself on Tillich, Dr. Robinson criticizes the traditional Christian teaching that God is a being, as it were, over against the world, a separate existence which has to be demonstrated. The sciences have no need of a God hypothesis, but there can be a sort of 'naturalist religion' in which we are to harmonize ourselves with the evolutionary process as it develops even higher forms of self-consciousness.

The theologian in Dr. Robinson wakes up at this point and hastens to point out that this means that the word 'God' is simply another name for the evolving universe, the totality of things as it moves forward, and is therefore semantically superfluous. But the God thus eliminated is only the God of supranaturalist Christian thinking. Need we be tied to such thinking even if it be the thinking of the Bible? Perhaps Sir Julian Huxley, with his evolutionary religion without a God 'out there,' is performing a valuable function, as valuable as that of his grandfather whose attacks on certain traditional interpretations helped the Church to a new understanding of the early chapters of Genesis?

The question is answered by a quotation from Bultmann, but here the theologian in Dr. Robinson again steps forward and we are given three weighty cautions about Bultmann. Watch this fellow! Then surprisingly comes a quotation from Bonhoeffer pointing out that the real trouble about Bultmann is that he does not go far enough. It is not sufficient to get rid of the miracles—which is what most ordinary people think about when you talk of the 'supranatural'— both the miracles and God must be understood and proclaimed in a 'non-religious sense.' But what does this mean? A long quotation from Bonhoeffer's *Letters from Prison* is then given to elucidate what is meant by a non-religious understanding of God; but it does not in fact succeed in explaining anything of the kind because of Dr. Robinson's studious refusal to define his terms. A question where the terms used are ambiguous or vague or simply not defined at all cannot be answered.

One of many defects of this book is that the words 'religion,' 'religious' and 'non-religious' are bandied about for no fewer than 86 pages (out of a total of 141!) before we are treated to a definition of 'religion,' and when we do get it, it is placed in a footnote, where the author coolly remarks 'this is perhaps (!!) the point to recognize that so much of the discussion for and against "religion" is bound to be a matter of definition.' First he quotes Tillich's definition of religion as 'not a special function of man's spiritual life but is the dimension of depth in all its functions.'[1] Dr. Robinson thinks this is right 'but I have preferred to retain the customary usage in order to bring out the point of Bonhoeffer's critique.' Yet we are still left with no definition of the customary usage, while a glance at a dictionary will show the inquisitive just what an elastic term 'religion' is.

More than half the rest of the chapter is taken up with quotations mainly from Bonhoeffer, the theme of which is that God is no longer needed as a hypothesis in science; that in most other spheres of life, too, He is not required; and that the realm of ultimate questions such as death and guilt, where the Church can make use of God, is probably shrinking too. We must in Bonhoeffer's words 'discard the religious premise.' There is no God of the sort that we can use, a *deus ex machina*. What the Bible gives us is a God who suffers—St. Paul's weakness and foolishness of God in fact.[2] But this profound thought is not followed up, for the object of this chapter is 'clearing the decks'—getting rid of allegedly fake conceptions of God in order to erect something better in their place.

The remainder of the chapter is devoted to a discussion of the transcendence of God. This has been understood traditionally as belief in a God as a supreme Person above or outside the world. It is this God whom the atheists like Huxley, the linguistic philosophers and the 'anti-theists' like Feuerbach and Nietzsche rejected. 'Can He be rehabilitated,' asks our author, 'or is the whole conception of that sort of a God, "up there," "out there" or however one likes

[1] H.T.G. p. 86 second footnote.
[2] I Corinthians *1*.25.

to put it, a projection, an idol, that can and should be torn down?'[1] The bishop, while rejecting an extreme statement of Dr. John Wren-Lewis to the effect that the whole of the traditional way of thinking about God is wrong, for, as the bishop says, it has served and can still serve some people, is yet convinced that it can be the greatest obstacle to an intelligent faith. 'We shall eventually be no more able to convince men of the existence of a God "out there," whom they must call in to order their lives, than persuade them to take seriously the gods of Olympus.'[2] This, however, does not mean substituting the idea of an immanent God for a transcendent one. On the contrary, the task is to validate the idea of transcendence for modern man. This is set forth in the chapter *The Ground of our Being*.

It may be asked if God is not 'out there' where is He? The answer is that God is not *another* Being at all, but the infinite depth and ground of *all* being. Following Tillich's advice we must forget everything traditional that we have learned about God, 'perhaps even the word itself.'[3] Martin Buber speaks of the person who with his lips denies God and believes himself to be godless. But when he 'gives his whole being to addressing the *Thou* of his life as a *Thou* that cannot be limited by another, he addresses God.'[4]

This is all extremely confused. To address anything whatsoever, especially something possessing personal attributes, which is *not* oneself is precisely to address another being. Everything that is not I is 'outside' myself. Of course if what I address is myself or even the depth of myself then I am talking to myself. It would be interesting to see this new version of Christianity being proclaimed to the Hindus.

[1] H.T.G. p. 41.
[2] H.T.G. p. 43.
[3] H.T.G. p. 47.
[4] H.T.G. p. 48.

'Man,' says the Swami Vivekananda, 'is an infinite circle whose circumference is nowhere but the centre is located on one spot, and God is an infinite circle whose circumference is nowhere, but whose centre is everywhere.'

There is some praise of Feuerbach as 'in a real sense right' when he wanted to translate theology into anthropology; and apparently Bultmann, in answer to a challenge from Karl Barth, admitted freely that he was doing the same thing.

But suddenly on the brink, the theologian in Dr. Robinson wakes up again and we are told that 'we are here on very dangerous ground.' Of course we are—the deification of man, to which Dr. Robinson has up to this point been steadily leading us. Which reminds him that John Macmurray is here equally unsound.

We are therefore brought back again to Tillich. We are not to deify the universe—if God is simply a name for everything we are pantheists. We are not to deify man— we should then be disciples of Feuerbach (and of course *he* in his turn might land us up inside the Marxist camp!— who knows? Back in the thirties I must confess I myself had just this idea of presenting the dialectic of history—the immanent force not ourselves making for righteousness—as another name for God. Here is another set of people nearer the kingdom of God than they imagine. The Bishop of Woolwich's position is wide open to infiltration from both the Hindu and the Marxist front!).

How then, at last, having abolished a God 'out there'; having refused to become pantheists, or monists with our Hindu and Marxist brothers; having declined the blandishments of Julian Huxley's religion without God, do we manage to preserve the idea of transcendence? In Tillich's words 'the finite world points beyond itself. In other words it is self-transcendent.' 'This,' goes on the bishop, 'I believe, is Tillich's great contribution to theology—the re-interpretation of transcendence in a way which preserves its reality while detaching it from the projection of supra-naturalism.'[1] This is quite meaningless. If there is nothing 'outside,' the finite world is pointing 'beyond itself' (Tillich) to nothing.

As might be expected, the section on God in the Bible is far more intelligible. I myself maintain that the categories of Holy Scripture so abused in this book, precisely because they are 'period pieces,' are far more adequate to handle this problem of God's transcendence (outside and above us) and immanence (within man and especially within the spirit-created community) than the contradictory and obscure notions hitherto set before us by the bishop. The paradoxes of the Bible, unlike those tortuosities of the Teutonic theologians with whom we have so far been inflicted, are clear and challenging. Incidentally, *why* does Dr. Robinson (who is not a scientist) imagine that science-trained people find his chosen mentors so illuminating? The odd thing is that, so often, the scientists who *are* Christians are orthodox. Could it be that they prefer a precise concrete language which, even if it needs translating, at least has a definable sense to start with?

[1]H.T.G. p. 56.

3

THE MAN FOR OTHERS

'THE doctrine of the Incarnation and Divinity of Christ is, on any count, central to the entire Christian message, and crucial therefore for any re-interpretation of it.'[1] The usual (and correct) things are said about the attempt of the Council of Chalcedon to define the belief of Christians that in the One Christ are two natures, human and divine; and the usual (and correct) things are also said about the constant tendency of popular devotion and popular theology to assert Christ's divinity at the expense of His humanity.

But of course as God (according to the new teaching) is no longer 'out there' (literally or otherwise) He cannot 'come down' at Christmas. The Christmas story, apart from the historical fact that the man Jesus was born, is simply a myth, which indicates 'the significance of the events, the divine depth of history. And we shall be grievously impoverished if our ears cannot tune to the angels' song or our eyes are blind to the wise men's star.

'But we must be able to read the nativity story without assuming that its truth depends on there being a literal interruption of the natural by the supernatural, that Jesus

[1]H.T.G. p. 64.

can only be Emmanuel—God with us—if, as it were, He came through from another world.'[1]

Perhaps the best comment on this is some words of Bonhoeffer himself in one of his last letters, not to his friend but to his parents, written at Christmastide 1943. 'That misery, suffering, poverty, loneliness, helplessness and guilt look very different to the eyes of God from what they do to man, *that God should come down* to the very place which men usually abhor, that Christ was born in a stable because there was no room for him in the inn—these are things which a prisoner can understand better than anyone else' (*Letters and Papers from Prison* Fontana edition p. 36. (My italics).

Nevertheless the bishop (rightly) will have nothing to do with a purely naturalistic view of Jesus Christ. Like Kierkegaard, he will not put Christ on 'the same level as those who have no authority, on the same level as geniuses, poets and thinkers.'[2] Athanasius again was correct in the stand he took for the full meaning of Christ as 'of one substance with the Father'—albeit that the saint's categories were at fault according to the new theology!

Into some of the technicalities of New Testament criticism, raised by the question of the claims made by Christ for Himself it is unnecessary to enter here, for they do not affect the main argument. I do not myself see for example that the more accurate translation of the opening verse of St. John's Gospel given by the bishop affects the main issue about the Person of Christ; and in any case New Testament Christology does not hang on a few isolated texts.

The bishop (I think because he is dealing with the Bible, the field in which he has really distinguished himself) is

[1]H.T.G. p. 68.
[2]'Of the Difference between a Genius and an Apostle' in *The Present Age* (Eng. tr. 1940) pp. 146 f. quoted by Dr. Robinson, p. 69.

quite clear that Jesus Christ cannot be explained on a purely naturalistic hypothesis. 'When one met Him (Jesus) one was met—and saved and judged—by God.'

Far and away the greatest things in this book are what the Bishop has to say about Christ as the final revelation of God and how the Godhead is manifested in Christ's complete giving or emptying of Himself which found its culminating point on the Cross. In these pages (71—75) there is a sureness of touch which is far to seek elsewhere in this book. The very *atmosphere* of these pages is different.

The last section of the chapter we have been discussing is headed *What is Christ for us Today?* It certainly begins well with two magnificent quotations from Bonhoeffer. Both these are needed, for the former one with its exclusive concern with what St. Paul called 'the weakness and foolishness of God' tells us nothing of the Resurrection. In the second the Resurrection is specifically mentioned, but nothing is worked out, for these are only notes for a book the writing of which the noose of a Nazi hangman has for ever prevented.

As Bonhoeffer speaks of God allowing himself to be edged out of the world and of God's 'powerlessness' we are reminded of one of the main themes of the philosophy of the Russian Orthodox Nicholas Berdyaev who in a memorable phrase said that God has less power than a policeman. For Berdyaev, like Bonhoeffer, had personal experience of the power exercised by the prince of this world, and he too was imprisoned more than once.

Dr. Robinson then develops Bonhoeffer's thought about 'God in human form.' Jesus the man 'existing for others and hence the Crucified.' It is this 'life for others through participation in the Being of God [which] *is* transcendence.'[1]

[1] H.T.G. p. 76.

And again 'the life of God, the ultimate Word of Love in which all things cohere, is bodied forth completely, unconditionally and without reserve in the life of a man—the man for others and the man for God.'[1]

This is the at-one-ment, but 'the whole schema of a supernatural Being coming down from heaven to 'save' mankind from sin, in the way a man might put his finger into a glass of water to rescue a struggling insect, is frankly incredible to man "come of age" who no longer believes in such a *deus ex machina*[2] ... At no point does the supranaturalist scheme appear less compelling. And yet at no point is the naturalistic view, even in its Liberal Christian form, shallower or more discredited than in its estimate of what is wrong with the world and of what is required to put it right. The case for pushing beyond them both to a third alternative is very urgent.'[3] Two long and excellent quotations from Tillich follow which speak in non-theological or perhaps it would be more accurate to say non-traditional, language of man's condition of estrangement from the Ground of Being from which he yet cannot escape, and of the gracious experience of acceptance entirely unmerited and unearned which can break in, in healing and light upon our darkest moments of despair and self-disgust. Tillich goes on to say how 'in the light of this grace we perceive the power of grace in our relation *to others and to ourselves.*' (My italics).

This, says Dr. Robinson, is what the Christian community exists for, to embody this new being as love and 'not to promote a new religion.' He then returns again to Bonhoeffer, and says that this means 'participation in the

[1]H.T.G. p. 77.
[2]H.T.G. p. 78.
[3]H.T.G. p. 79.

powerlessness of God in the world.' I find this somewhat of a *non-sequitur*. His quotation from Bonhoeffer is tantalizing in its mixture of sharply-etched challenging profundity, and the obscurity which arises from terms not defined, and the inevitable incompleteness of oracles given to the world by divers portions under the frightening conditions in which Bonhoeffer spent the last years of his life.

'Christians range themselves with God in His suffering; that is what distinguishes them from the heathen. As Jesus asked, "Could ye not watch with me one hour?" That is the exact opposite of what the religious man expects from God . . . It is not some religious act which makes a Christian what he is, but participation in the suffering of God in the life of the world.'[1]

But St. Paul, who also had known imprisonment and misfortune of beatings and stonings, says 'that I may know Him (Christ) and the power of His Resurrection and the fellowship of His sufferings.'[2] In general, has Western Christianity, whether Protestant or Catholic, put the New Testament *emphasis* on the Resurrection?

Bonhoeffer's words here were wrung out of him by a real participation in Gethsemane. This is a real 'moment' of Christian living in one form or another. But it is *not* the whole gospel, as Bonhoeffer would have been the first to admit. New Testament Christianity is 'crucifixion-resurrection'—crucifixion in this aeon 'in which we see not yet all things subjected to Him'—resurrection in the coming aeon . . . And if this be not supranaturalism, then words have no meaning!

[1] Quoted from Bonhoeffer. H.T.G. p. 82.
[2] Philippians 3.10.

4

WORLDLY HOLINESS

IF, as Bonhoeffer says, 'it is not some religious act which makes a Christian what he is, but participation in the suffering of God in the life of the world,'[1] then what place or meaning have either worship or prayer? A consideration of this at last compels Dr. Robinson to define the terms 'religion' and 'religious.' The religious sphere is opposed to the secular.

The outstanding features of this religious sphere are private and public prayers, worship—church services, sacraments, Bible-reading and meditation at home, retreats, quiet-days etc. In other words the religious sphere, in this sense, is a department of life. We go apart from ordinary life to seek God. That is the essence of religion. The holy is precisely that which is not common. To quote our author, this is 'the Jewish priestly conception of the relation of the sacred to the secular which was shattered by the Incarnation, when God declared all things holy, and the veil of the temple was rent from top to bottom.'[2]

Surely this is an extraordinarily loose bit of writing from the pen of a very accomplished Biblical scholar! To begin

[1]Quoted on p. 83, H.T.G.
[2]H.T.G. p. 87.

with, the rending of the veil of the temple was one of those profound wordless events which is full of more meanings than one. So far as the category of the holy is concerned, the rending of the veil surely means, not that the holy is abolished, but that the way into the holy is now open for Jew and Gentile, bond and free, without the mediation of the priesthood of the Old Covenant. We may also remember that, so far from abolishing the category of the holy, Christ Himself said 'Give not that which is holy unto the dogs, neither cast ye your pearls before swine.'[1]

But when Dr. Robinson goes on to expound what worship means he has some very good and very clear things to say, though (as he himself would be the first to admit) things which others also have said. In-growing religiosity is certainly with us and cannot be too often exposed, as many a parish priest ought constantly to be doing. It must, for example, be nearly forty years ago since Bishop Frank Weston of Zanzibar at an Anglo-Catholic Congress said to his hearers (the exact wording escapes me): 'You have been adoring Christ in the Blessed Sacrament, now go out and find Him in the slums!' What is said in *Honest to God* about the Eucharist, and about the 'holiness' in the 'common,' is all well said, and very much to the point.

But why here and all through the book use the words 'religion' and 'religious' to mean only *spurious religiosity*? This Pickwickian use of everyday words is of course the besetting sin of 'Oxbridge,' and I say this not as an 'outsider' with a chip on his shoulder, but as one who has had seven happy years both of junior and senior Oxford life. Dons, like other workers of hand and brain, have their occupational diseases. They are apt to lose the common touch, and never more perilously than when they imagine that

[1]St. Matt. 7.6.

they at least are not as other dons are—'remote and
ineffectual,' as certain also of our own poets have said.

One of the by-products of this condition is this itch to
use ordinary words in extraordinary senses without apparently a thought for what this can mean to the man in the
street; especially when such utterances are torn from their
context and hurled about by the 'means of mass communication' ever hungry for sensation. It is not too much to say
that in *Honest to God* religion becomes a 'dirty word.' An
incredible amount of harm must have been done by this to
simple people, believers and unbelievers, who have not yet
forgotten (maybe) the equally irresponsible use of the
words 'holy communion' during Dr. Robinson's defence of
Lady Chatterley's Lover.

It is all very well talking about finding God in personal
relationships in the real world. The real world is not the
hortus inclusus of 'Oxbridge' with its own 'freemasonry,'
its vogue words and (dare one say it?) clichés. Rather is
it a baffling assortment of educated, uneducated and semi-
educated persons. A good deal more thought and care is
needed before one addresses oneself to such a multitude,
as one assuredly does when one writes paper-backs. What
for example, can ordinary people be expected to make of
such a sentence as the following? 'And, unless—against all
the protests of the religious—the Church can discover and
stand for a different conception of worship "in an entire
absence of religion", it too is set for decline and fall.'[1]

The last section of this chapter is called *A 'Non-religious'
Understanding of Prayer.* It is, with the pages on Christology, easily one of the best and most enlightening parts
of the book, though it contains some bits of advice which
even the author has to admit are dangerous. The quota-

[1]H.T.G. p. 91.

tions from Dr. George Macleod's *Only One Way Left* are stimulating, and avoid some of the exaggerations of the bishop, which obscure rather than throw into sharp relief what he is trying to say.

There can be no doubt whatsoever that both the former moderator and the bishop have put their fingers on a real problem. The prayer-life of the Church, and especially of the clergy, is too exclusively modelled on that of the cloister, of monks and nuns. Nicholas Berdyaev, when he returned to the Church, said exactly the same thing; he wanted 'a new spirituality' in the world. Historically, monasticism was the answer to the acute secularisation of the Church which followed the State recognition of Christianity by Constantine. The world invaded the Church, so the monks and nuns fled into the wilderness; and it would be quite impossible to estimate all that the cloister has meant, and does mean, for the Church when it is true to its principles. Those who live in monasteries are the specialists, the experts in prayer, and to them the clergy and laity who are 'in the world' have looked for guidance. But, in fact, are the ways of praying and of meditating worked out in the cloister always and at all times suitable for those who live 'in the world'? I think Dr. Robinson is probably inclined to over-emphasise the numbers of those, especially among the clergy, who do not find help in this direction, but they undoubtedly exist.

This is a point in *Honest to God* which needs seriously following up and discussing. Dr. Robinson has been quite wrongly accused of denying the need of periods of withdrawal for prayer, but his habit of over-stating his case and then qualifying his over-statement is no doubt responsible for this untrue criticism.

All that he has to say about meeting God in personal

contacts with others for whom one feels ultimate concern is true, and there are times when withdrawal for prayer has to be surrendered for active concern for another. For example, if one is a hospital chaplain where, owing to the rapid turnover of patients, one can never minister to all adequately, the tension between times of withdrawal and times of immersion with people is something one lives with every day; and it is a tension which can become acute.

But the bishop's suggestion that prayer should be decided by consideration not of *chronos* (clock-time) but of *kairos* (the moment when you *must* pray) is not at all wise, especially in the modern world with its endless interruptions. And this is said not simply in deference to what our best spiritual guides have said but is very much (so far as the present writer is concerned) a matter of practical experience. There seem to have been occasions when there was no leisure for Jesus and the disciples even to eat, let alone to pray. They experienced the overcrowded and over-demanding environment, even in Galilee.

But then we read also of those nights spent in withdrawal and prayer. In other words you may not always be able to keep to your disciplined rhythm of withdrawal and immersion; indeed, God may call you from it through the needs of others; but a disciplined rhythm there must be . . . But *as to the way we pray* here the exploring of new methods is of first-class importance.

And what after all *is* prayer? The classic definition is that prayer is the lifting up of the heart, mind and will to God. It is a Godward activity. The definition of prayer on page 100 of this book is therefore most inadequate. 'Prayer,' says Dr. Robinson, 'is the responsibility to meet others with *all* I have, to be ready to encounter the unconditional in the conditional, to expect to meet God in the way, not to turn aside from the way.' To which one can only reply frankly that it all depends on what the way is.[1] It is true that he that loveth not his brother whom he hath seen cannot love God whom he hath not seen.[2] An individualistic piety, bent on its own salvation and without a real self-giving love for others, a real involvement in others, is by New Testament standards a deceiving of ourselves.

It is true that in deep concern for others we meet God, we should look for Him and expect Him. It is also true that many who would call themselves atheists, and who never say prayers, spend and are spent in selfless *agape* for others. It is true that in the 'parable' of the Sheep and the Goats (though primarily concerned with something more particular) Jesus Himself points to this truth. (Incidentally, there should certainly be plenty of communists in Heaven and perhaps, after the late Pope John's last encyclical, more Christians will be thinking along these lines.) Nevertheless, 'being for others' is *not* all that can be said about prayer; and for those who have seen God in Jesus Christ 'prayer' in the common or garden sense of the word—withdrawing to pray—is inescapably necessary.

[1] The references in this chapter to the Damascus Road and the Emmaus Road are puzzling. The future St. Paul was not 'in the way' on any 'ultimate concern' for other people. He was 'in the way' to arrest, to beat up and perhaps to kill. Our Lord caught him, as it were, red-handed. The relevance of this to prayer, and how far prayer is simply a deep concern for others, would not appear to be immediately obvious. Similarly with the Emmaus Road, Cleopas and his friend were running away from it all when Christ met them . . . Really, Dr. Robinson!
[2] I John 4.20.

5

'THE NEW MORALITY'

FROM prayer we pass on to ethics. Even ten years ago it would have been hard to imagine a bishop writing this chapter. Today it is less surprising. It is probably the worst chapter in the book.

There is, we are told, a moral revolution taking place today which has reached gale-force. (Incidentally, it is a pity that both those who rejoice in this, and those who deplore it, share a strange lack of interest in discovering in precisely what parts of the world and in what classes of society this revolution operates, and to what degree. If such research were undertaken it might modify considerably our estimate as to its proper significance).

However, there *is* this revolution and 'Christianity is identified *tout court* with the old, traditional morality. That would not matter if this morality were Christian.'[1] No doubt, says the bishop, it 'served the Church in its day and still seems perfectly adequate—and indeed vitally necessary—to the religious'—without quotes this time; meaning those benighted second-class Christians who, according to Dr. Robinson, are on the way out.

To these traditionalists right and wrong are

[1]H.T.G. p. 106.

commandments laid down by God—something 'given'.
Certain things are always sins. (The bishop takes as an
example the question of divorce, but for the present we will
put on one side the discussion of this particular problem,
since it would interrupt the main thread of the argument.
We shall return to it later). Clearly a morality based on
God's commands can only be relevant to those who believe
in God. In an age when so many do not believe, the relevance of a morality with a supernatural foundation is restricted in its appeal.[1]

But this, Dr. Robinson tells us, is not the most fundamental criticism which can be made of supranaturalistic
ethics. The real *gravamen* lies in the fact that they distort
the teaching of our Lord Jesus Christ. Christ did not lay
down precepts which were binding at all times and in all
places, insisting that certain actions were always wrong and
others always right. The Sermon on the Mount, for example,
is not a new Law; its precepts are not the cast-iron regula-
tions of a code but 'illustrations of what love may at any
moment require of anyone.'[2]

Of course this is true of many things in the Sermon on
the Mount. Such sayings as 'give to him that asketh of
thee.'[3] are obviously not rules which can be literally observed by everyone on every possible occasion; and no
properly trained moral theologian has ever supposed that
they were. It is abundantly clear that much of the moral
teaching of Jesus was given in this form, and there is nothing
either 'new' or 'revolutionary' in recognizing this.

But it is totally incorrect to say that *all* the moral teaching of Jesus is on these lines. In the Sermon on the Mount,

[1]See p. 110 H.T.G.
[2]*Ibid.*
[3]St. Matt. 5.42.

2

for example, murder, adultery and perjury are clearly regarded by our Lord as actions which are always wrong, in any circumstances and in any place, and the whole point of this teaching was to show how much more deeply they should be understood. Or again, granted that the woman taken in adultery was not condemned, she was definitely told to 'go and sin no more.'[1] And what on the bishop's conception of Christ's teaching are we to make of Mark 7.21-23? 'For from within, out of the heart of men, evil thoughts proceed, fornications (in modern English, sexual relationships outside marriage), thefts, murders, adulteries, covetings, wickednesses, deceit, lasciviousness, an evil eye, railing, pride, foolishness : *all these evil things* proceed from within and defile the man.' (Which is also perhaps why some of us who are realistic are interested precisely in a God 'outside,' and hope and believe that such a God does exist !).

Christ Himself tells us that He came to *fulfil* the Law not *to abolish it*,[2] and St. Paul (Romans 13.10) also reminds us that love is the fulfilling of the Law. The commandments are *comprehended not abolished* when they are summed up in the words 'Thou shalt love thy neighbour as thyself.' The whole subject of the relation between the gracious absolutes of the Sermon on the Mount and the Law is handled in a most illuminating and stimulating way by Nicholas Berdyaev in the magnificent section on *Morality on this Side of Good and Evil* in *The Destiny of Man*. Here he divides up his subject under three headings, *The Ethics of Law, The Ethics of Redemption,* and *The Ethics of Creativity*; concluding with a chapter on concrete ethical problems. He can, in his own way, be as startling

[1] St. John *8*.11.
[2] Matt. *5*.17.

as Dr. Robinson; he can say some very harsh things about 'abstract norms' for instance, but he keeps his head. He sees far more clearly than Dr. Robinson the essential role of Law, even for a Christian.

To return now to the specific question of marriage and divorce. I am certain that Dr. Robinson is absolutely and entirely right when he repudiates the idea that Christ was legislating on this subject. But surely he knows that one can say that without attacking the whole system of super-natural ethics? Apart from a passing, unkind reference to the Russian Church on p. 138 one would never guess from reading this book that a thing called Eastern Orthodoxy existed. If Dr. Robinson had been more aware of these great Churches of the East, and their peculiar contribution, so different in texture even from either Protestantism or Roman Catholicism, he would have realized that it is per-fectly possible to apply Christ's teaching on marriage and divorce in a far more understanding way than either Roman Catholicism or (present-day) Anglicanism do.

The Orthodox, indeed, have a deeper understanding of the ideal of marriage as a life-long indissoluble union than the West, which is symbolized in the reduced ceremonial when a widow or widower marries again. But they have precisely what Dr. Robinson pleads for, a clear perception of the individual situation. They recognize, quite realistic-ally, that marriages do in fact fail, and that the granting of a divorce may in certain cases be closer to the mind of Christ than to maintain the letter of the law.

One last comment on this chapter. Towards the end we find certain qualifications appearing—another of Dr. Robinson's after-thoughts. It appears that after all it is *not* enough to say 'love God, and *then* what you will, do.' 'Such an ethic cannot but rely, in deep humility, upon guiding rules, upon the cumulative experience of one's own and other people's obedience. It is this bank of experience which gives us our working rules of 'right' and 'wrong' *and without them we could not but flounder*.[1] Exactly! And surely this should have been said at the beginning of the chapter.

The bishop protests that he is misunderstood, to which it can only be replied that his method of pursuing some extreme proposition (fortified by long quotations from other writers) over several pages, before he produces his qualifications, is asking for trouble. Nor, in this particular case, has he gone far enough in qualification. The 'working rules' (to use his expression) do not merely come from other people's experience. The most important ones, as has already been shown, come from Jesus Christ Himself.

[1]H.T.G. pp. 119, 120. Italics mine.

6

RECASTING THE MOULD

D R. ROBINSON'S last chapter begins with another quotation from Bonhoeffer in which he says '... if we reach a stage of being radically without religion—and I think this is the case already, else how is it, for instance, that this war, unlike any of those before it, is not calling forth any "religious" reaction?—what does that mean for Christianity?

It means that the linchpin is removed from the whole structure of our Christianity to date.'

The bishop then tries to elucidate this but ends up with 'I am not sure yet whether we can fully understand the question, let alone give the answer' . . . Then why ask it? If one must write a book full of quotations, full of undefined and variously defined terms, at least one might attempt to make them intelligible. However we have certainly got a fitting introduction to what is (apart from the last two or three pages) the most incoherent chapter in the whole book.

The bishop, baffled (as we are) by the quotation from Bonhoeffer, sets himself a more limited aim, that is 'to consider the implications of what he has been saying for our present "pattern of religion".[1] This pattern is for most people, we are told, indistinguishable from the Gospel itself. But unless the pattern which belongs to a past age can be remoulded, unless we can re-cast our thinking, Christianity will be abandoned.

We are given, as an analogy to the sort of remoulding needed, St. Paul's attitude to the Law of Moses. The Law was good, it was of divine origin; but in the end it became a 'stumbling-block to knowing the very God whose truth it existed to shape.'[2] However, Dr. Robinson is himself a bit unhappy about the relevance of this particular analogy for, as he points out, St. Paul's problem was precisely *not re-moulding an old Gospel but preaching a new one*. May not the choice of this analogy be itself due to a subconscious doubt in the mind of Dr. Robinson as to whether after all the remoulded Gospel now offered for our acceptance is really the original article and not 'another' or a 'different' gospel?[3] ... There are so many second thoughts in this little book!

We must then re-mould, or Christianity will without doubt perish, the contents of the parcel will disappear with the wrapping. But 'once again, we must insist, there is nothing wrong as such with the God of the religious premise, with "the One above" to whom the religious person instinctively "turns"—provided he be truly the God and Father of our Lord. . . . Such a religious pattern holds for him "the very shape of knowledge and truth"—and woe betide the one who would wantonly shatter it.'[4] Yet, only twelve lines further on, we are told, with reference to the necessary re-moulding, that we must 'be prepared for *everything* to go

[1]H.T.G. p. 123.
[2]*Ibid*.
[3]Galatians *1*.6, 7.
[4]H.T.G. p. 124.

into the melting—even our most cherished religious categories and moral absolutes. And the first thing we must be ready to let go is our image of God himself.'[1]

It is difficult to write temperately about such an amazing jumble of contradictions coming from a man who has spent most of his adult life teaching students. The 2,000 year-old framework of Christianity *must* be broken up if Christianity is to survive, nevertheless this framework is all right for second-class Christians who are still 'religious,' and woe betide if we shatter it! But of course *everything* (*sic*) must go into the melting, the image of God first!

People often admire the glorious comprehensiveness of the Church of England, and you certainly have it here. (Or is this what Marxists call 'the union of opposites'?). One thing, however, is obvious if the bishop's policy of melting and re-moulding is to be implemented, a new race of bi-lingual clergy will be a top priority, chosen adepts whose double-talk and double-cross, as they shuttle to and fro between melted and unmelted groups of Christians, will need in the background a weight of learning and an elasticity of mind which our present theological colleges seem hardly likely to impart!

It is *of course* true that men may come to worship their own ideas of God rather than the living God Himself; that there may be mental as well as metal idols, and that thought may petrify. But surely it is one of the main functions of the Christian preacher to be continually awakening himself and his hearers to the living content of the images, symbols, formulae, rites and ceremonies of religion. And the source of such continual awakening is the Holy Spirit. But, to change the metaphor, 'other foundation can no man lay than that which is laid, which is Jesus Christ.'[2] The

[1] *Ibid.*
[2] 1 Cor. 3.11.

Image of the invisible God is Christ[1] and anyone who throws *that* Image into the melting has ceased to be a Christian!

I, like the bishop, have great sympathy with some atheists, and probably know as many as he does. I agree that some are rebelling, not against the true God, but against false conceptions of Him. I agree that many will be set on the Right Hand at the Last Day who never 'saw' Christ.[2] But it is a complete confusion of thought to argue from this, *not modern but primitive*, gospel truth that therefore our Image of God must be scrapped. I repeat, the Image cannot be scrapped if we are to remain Christians; for that Image is Christ Himself.

But what is all this image-scrapping in aid of? What is the object of the exercise? Not, apparently, as one might expect, in the interests of some newer, higher and more compelling truth. If that were so it would clearly be quite immoral to encourage those satisfied with the 'old image' to continue their devotions along the old lines If a new truth wipes out the old, and you see the new truth, then you have no business as a responsible teacher to go on encouraging what you know to be false. That would be promoting superstition with a vengeance! But the bishop has already said a 'woe betide' to those who would wantonly shatter a religious pattern which holds for others 'the very shape of knowledge and truth.' Indeed the bishop himself (or part of him) can still speak of the old image of God as being 'as much my God as theirs'![3]

No. The call to image-smashing comes not from the discovery of some new truth which must cancel out the old. It is the call 'to help men through to the conviction about

[1]Col. *1*.15.
[2]St. Matt. *25*.37.
[3]H.T.G. p. 126.

ultimate Reality that alone finally matters.' In other words the motive is pedagogical; it is an attempt to discover a more efficient means of imparting truth to those not prepared to accept the Christian Faith as normally presented.

And what is this truth that the Bishop wants to impart? That 'there is nothing in death or life . . . in the world as it is or the world as it shall be, in the forces of the universe, in heights or depths—nothing in all creation that can separate us from the love of God in Christ Jesus our Lord.'[1] . . . 'That,' says the bishop, 'I believe with all my being, and that is what at heart it means to be a Christian.'

How can he then go on *in the very next sentence* to say, 'as for the rest, as for the images of God, whether metal or mental, I am prepared to be an agnostic with the agnostics, even an atheist with the atheists?'[2]

I said earlier that parts of Dr. Robinson's book are heretical, but on reflection I want to withdraw that adjective. Heresy, after all, *is* an attempt to develop logically or redefine in clearer terms some aspect of 'the faith once delivered to the saints.' A great deal of this book is not heresy, but just 'non-sense'! It is about time someone said so.

The trouble is that Dr. Robinson has hopelessly confused two quite different things. It is one thing to go to those outside the Christian Faith, who misunderstand it, perhaps, because it has been crudely presented to them in childhood, and to seek to interpret to such people their deepest intuitions of Ultimate Reality, laying aside, during such dialogue, all the images which Christians normally use. Of course such a method is valid and much of the best missionary work in non-Christian countries is done on similar lines. It is quite another thing to say in general terms that Christians must

[1] Romans *8*.38 . (NEB.).
[2] H.T.G. p. 127.

scrap their image of God or go under. As the war-time poster put it. 'Careless talk costs lives.'

Dr. Robinson now goes on to guard his 'position' (*sic*) on two flanks.[1] He deals with non-Christian naturalism, and then 'orthodox' supranaturalism. For the former he selects Sir Julian Huxley as the protagonist.

Huxley, Bonhoeffer (and the bishop himself?) are at one in discarding the supranaturalist framework. 'But where Huxley does it in the interest of religion without revelation (surely without God, too. O.F.C.) Bonhoeffer does it in the interests of Christianity without religion—not, of course, that Bonhoeffer desires to abolish religion (then why say that he does? O.F.C.), in the way that Huxley wants to dispense with revelation : he simply wishes to free Christianity from any necessary dependence upon "the religious premise".'[2]

This oracle I leave to speak for itself . . . But in the next two pages we have a number of perfectly orthodox and straightforward statements. For example 'Christianity stands or falls by revelation, by Christ as the disclosure of the final truth not merely about human nature (that we might accept relatively easily) but about all nature and all reality. The Christian's faith cannot rest in the capacities of man.'[3] And that, of course, is where Huxley is criticized. The bishop speaks up for the traditional use of *homoousios* in connection with Christ which means that He is 'of one substance with the Father.' 'For unless the *ousia, the being,* of things deep down is Love, of the quality disclosed in the life, death and resurrection of Jesus Christ, then the Christian could have little confidence in affirming the ulti-

[1]H.T.G. p. 127.
[2]*Ibid.*
[3]H.T.G. p. 128.

mate personal character of reality. And this—not his religiosity, nor his belief in the existence of a Person in heaven—is what finally distinguishes him from the humanist and the atheist.'[1]

I am afraid I find the idea of a reality which is love, and therefore personal, but not a Person, pretty baffling. What is love but one person loving another? Love is not an abstraction—nor would one speak of the love of two atoms of hydrogen, though heaven knows they are deep down! Moreover the Christianity of the New Testament and of traditional theology does not say that God is *a* Person, but three Persons in one God.[2] The fully developed doctrine of the Church on the Trinity is simply the statement, in a formula, of the truths about God historically revealed in the New Testament. It is not a puzzle thought up by some Greek theologians who had nothing better to do than corrupt the simple faith.

It is noticeable too that it is only *after* God has revealed Himself as three Persons that St. John is able to produce the statement, God is love. For if God were simply *a* Person, Whom did He love, and in what conceivable sense was He love before the creation of man? Far be it from me to say that the doctrine about this (the profoundest of all matters) raises no problems, but it is at least more enlightening than some of this new theology. At least the terms employed are constants—unlike those twin chameleons 'religion' and 'religious' as they appear in this book, whose colour range must be the eighth wonder of the world!

Dr. Robinson then tries to defend himself against 'the representatives of traditional supernaturalism.'[3] These in-

[1]H.T.G. p. 129.
[2]The bishop himself refers to this on pp. 39f.
[3]H.T.G. p. 130.

clude, of course, the vast mass of Christians both past and present of all sections of the Church, from the Romans at one end to the Plymouth Brethren at the other, the writers of the New Testament, and finally and above all our Lord Jesus Christ Himself, who never talked anything else but the language of supernaturalism and of a Father in Heaven.

Our author feels he may be accused of pantheism. For in pantheism too there is no God 'outside,' 'above' or 'in the depth.' Everything *is* God. There can be no morality in such a system for 'I am the slayer *and* the slain.' But as Dr. Robinson says 'We are not like rays to the sun or leaves to the tree : we are united to the source, sustainer and goal of our life in a relationship whose only analogy is that of *I* to *Thou*—except that the freedom in which we are held is one of utter dependence.'[1] And later, 'it may be impossible to *imagine* the personal ground of all our being except as an almighty Individual, endowed with a centre of consciousness and will like ourselves and yet wholly "other".' As symbols these images have their powerful and proper place. They become idols only when the images are regarded as indispensable for the apprehending of reality.'[2] But we have just been told on the previous page that we are united to the source etc. of our life in a relationship whose only analogy is that of *I* and *Thou*! . . . Why then 'depth' is more helpful than 'height' when the *only* analogy of our relationship to it is I to Thou—heaven (or should we now say hell?) only knows.

Canon Hugh Montefiore's observation (quoted here) that 'our impasse is primarily an intellectual one' would appear to be a glimpse of the obvious. To add insult to

[1]H.T.G. p. 131.
[2]H.T.G. p. 132.

injury, the unfortunate reader who has got thus far is given some of the canon's words (on another subject) in *Soundings* which would apply equally well, so the bishop appears to suggest, to the matter now under discussion.

'It does not immediately or directly affect Christian faith or Christian worship or the conduct of the Christian life. God is still at work. The old formulas continue to be used . . . so long as the search can and does continue, the insufficiency of our theology need not affect Christian faith or conduct or worship.'[1] But such statements as '*the first thing* we must be ready to let go is our image of God himself' are the cry, not of the searcher, but of the iconoclast.

In the final section of his last chapter the Bishop sketches some consequences for the Church. One is wholly with him and with Dr. Vidler in their scathing criticism of the inward-looking departmentalized conception of religion which regards it as 'not concerned with the whole of life, but with a part of life . . .'[2] and underlines the need to 'increase our emphasis upon the church as a *religious* organization with a *limited* purpose.' On the contrary, as Bonhoeffer says, '*The Church is her true self only when she exists for humanity.*'[3] How true!

Nevertheless 'unless the Christian's "life is hid with Christ in God"[4] then any distinction between being *in* the world but not *of* it disappears, and at once he is down one side of the "knife-edge." There must be what Jacques Ellul has called a distinctively Christian "style of life" and if this is not nourished all is lost. Yet even this is best not described in religious terms as it is not confined to the sphere of religion. As Ellul, the layman, puts it, "the whole

[1]H.T.G. p. 133.
[2]H.T.G. p. 134.
[3]H.T.G. p. 135.
[4]Colossians 3.3.

of life is concerned" in it. "It includes the way we think about present political questions as well as our way of practising hospitality".[1] What Dr. Robinson envisages here is a life which combines prayer, worship and spiritual discipline with an all-out active concern with the whole of life about us, social, *political,* and no doubt cultural, though this is not specifically mentioned . . . And this would be wholeheartedly endorsed by numberless clergymen and laymen who are trying, however imperfectly, to do just this sort of thing; though they feel no need to get rid of their image of God as a first step. On the contrary, they would say that it is Christ as a Person 'out there,' the Image of the invisible God, who commands them to do exactly this—to be for others in the world.

This objective the bishop says 'could be put in another way by saying that the Church must become genuinely and increasingly *lay*—providing we understand that much misused word aright. For the laity are people of God, and the people of God are *for* the world.' He then goes on to quote Fr. Yves Congar who has defined a layman as 'one for whom the things of this world are "really interesting *in themselves*" for whom "their truth is not as it were swallowed up and destroyed by a higher reference"—for instance, by how far they can be turned to the service of the Church, or used as occasions for evangelism.'[2] This Fr. Congar calls a genuine 'laicity'; and, of course, it must not be confined only to those in the pews. The clergy must share in this temper. Yet Fr. Congar has not had to invent a new theology to say this.

A similar point was once made in another connection by

---

[1] *The Presence of the Kingdom* (1951) pp. 145-50 as quoted by Dr. Robinson. H.T.G. p. 136.
[2] H.T.G. p. 137.

Dorothy Sayers. In one of her plays a number of young men were needed to play the part of angels, and some good soul wrote saying that she hoped great care had been taken, before everything else, to see that they were pious. To which Dorothy Sayers replied that the first questions she asked were whether the young men could speak their lines, were physically fit enough to stand for some time holding up very heavy wings, and whether they would arrive on time, and arrive sober. The job for a job worth while *in itself* ... But, again, Dorothy Sayers was nothing if not orthodox!

One does not require a new image of God in order to be able to agree with Dr. Robinson when he says 'I would see much more hope for the Church if it was organized not to defend the interests of religion against the inroads of the state (legitimate and necessary as this may be) but to equip Christians, by the quality and powers of its community life to enter with their "secret discipline" into all the exhilarating and dangerous secular strivings of our day, there to follow, and to find, the workings of God.'[1]

Our Lord indeed saw the function of His disciples in terms of leaven in the lump, of salt, or of light shining in darkness.[2] Behind all these metaphors or analogies lies the idea of one thing mingling with another; one thing being lost in another, in order to change it for the better. The whole purpose of leaven, salt and light is *use*—'being for others.' But the salt is no good if it has lost its peculiar tang; and it *can* lose it when it is sufficiently adulterated. Light is no good if it is put under a bushel. One would therefore agree at once with the bishop that in the actual process of penetrating the 'world' the idiom need not be *at all times*

[1] H.T.G. p. 139.
[2] See, for example St. Matt. *13*.33 and St. Matt. *5*.13-16.

'religious' i.e. talk about God, about prayer, or about anything which we do or say in church.

I remember once returning to my hospital from leave and enquiring how a young priest who had been deputising for me had got on in a rather hard-boiled men's ward under (to put it mildly) a not very religious sister. The patient I asked replied quite simply and naturally, 'Oh he never said a word about religion but you just felt that Christ had been there!' 'Religionless Christianity' then after all? . . . But the priest in question was a very definite Anglo-Catholic. Not much doubt about his images!

Again, a few years ago I was in Russia with some 200 young British Christians, and we had arranged for some group discussions with Russian Christians, priests and lay people. One of the Britishers asked what Russian Christians did about 'social witness'—a term the Russians found it hard to understand at first. When this was explained to them they said (in effect) 'Well, we just get on with the job.' If a Christian feels that, say, housing or health in any locality needs attention, he will become a builder or seek election as a non-party member, or something like that; —in fact 'muck in' side-by-side with the people who are getting on with the actual job, in one way or another.

I found the same attitude from the communist side in a similar discussion with young Marxists and young Christians. A girl in a watch-factory said 'we've got two believers' —the usual word in Russia for anyone with religion—'in my shop on the same bench. We get on perfectly well together. They want to make the factory a success and so do we communists. There's no difference.' As a leading communist theoretician said to me 'after all, the New Russia has been built by believers as well as unbelievers.' Yet there is nothing 'religion-less' about a Russian Christian. Very much the reverse!

In a word, I find a false antithesis in this whole conception of 'religion-less Christianity.' The secular world, and its secular demands and activities, has its own worth, its own place, its own dignity and value as part of the creation of God. It has its peculiar laws and disciplines. Nevertheless it is *not* the whole; and the Christian with his religion has therefore a function within it which is not of this world, a world which still groans and which still, as in St. Paul's day, awaits redemption and 'the manifestation of the sons of God.'[1]

'Hold to Christ, and for the rest be totally uncommitted,'[2] wrote Herbert Butterfield; and the bishop quotes him with approval. But as I have already shown, many points in this new theology (which the bishop, to do him justice, has but half-digested) are not a holding to Christ, but a repudiation of Him. The bishop is right in saying that our job is to get alongside a largely religion-less world; and certainly we must learn to talk its language. But if we are *ourselves* religion-less then the salt has lost its savour. 'It is thenceforth good for nothing'[3]—'fit neither for the land nor for the dunghill. Men cast it out.'[4]

[1]Romans *8*.19-23.
[2]Quoted from *Christianity & History*, H.T.G. p. 140.
[3]St. Matthew *5*.13.
[4]St. Luke *14*.35.

PART TWO

The Christian Gospel in the Contemporary World

7

THE HEART OF THE GOSPEL

IN the second part of this book we shall be concerned with two things. Firstly, 'What is Christianity?' Secondly, 'What is the situation in which it has to exist, function, and propagate itself today?'

The order of the questions is extremely important. The trouble about many attempts to re-state Christianity or give it a new image is that they begin with the situation, and not with Christ. In Fr. Ronald Knox's *Some Loose Stones*[1] there was a chapter entitled 'How much will Jones swallow?' It is a perfectly legitimate question, but absolutely fatal when it is put first in any discussion of what Christianity can mean today.

What then is Christianity about? What primarily is it? Firstly, of course, it is about something which actually happened. There was the Man, Jesus. He Lived, He taught, He died, He rose again. 'But did He, in fact, rise again?' asks the unbeliever. A good question, because it goes to the heart of the matter. For if Jesus did not rise again from the dead, if 'crucified, dead and buried' were *in fact* the last words in the story of Jesus, if the end of Jesus was exactly the same as that of any other human being, the

[1]A reply to *Foundations*, written when Fr. Knox was still an Anglican.

task of explaining how Christianity ever came into being at all is a pretty difficult one.

The story of Jesus, if it ended on Good Friday, would be just one more example of what has been repeated millions and millions of times ever since the human race first emerged on this planet. Goodness is and has been continually 'crucified, dead and buried,' and what gospel is there in that? If there had been no Resurrection, all you could say truthfully about Jesus was what Thomas Hardy said about his most famous character, 'the President of the Immortals . . . had ended his sport with Tess.'

The Russian atheists have understood all this very clearly. If, for example, you go into what used to be the Cathedral of Our Lady of Kazan, in Leningrad, and is now the Museum of the History of Religion, you will see that Christ is presented as a myth. He is put on a level with the figures in Greek or Norse mythology—beings who never existed in history but were created by poetic imagination in order to shed light upon some of the ultimate questions about life that have always bothered mankind.

It is fashionable in the West to laugh at Christ-myth theories. Everybody here says, 'Of course there was once a man called Jesus;—the question is, was He divine, are half the said things about Him true, and above all did He rise from the dead? None of those questions are simple, and if you say 'no' to the last one the business of explaining how Christianity came into existence is a very, very difficult one, especially since the only evidence available asserts that He *did* in fact rise from the dead.

The Russian atheists—being good chess players no doubt, and therefore always a few moves ahead—have seen perfectly clearly where you land up when you admit the historical existence of Jesus but deny His resurrection. And so, very sensibly from their own point of view, they stick to the Christ-myth—a Jesus who had no historical existence, and is simply on a level with Diana or Woden.

Islam has also a sound instinct from its own standpoint when it asserts that Jesus did not die on the Cross. For, if there was no death, obviously there could be no resurrection.

It is not only, then, orthodox Christians, but their opponents too, who regard the Resurrection of Christ as the hinge on which Christianity turns. When the Athenian scoffers summed up the teaching of St. Paul in two words 'Jesus and the Resurrection'[1] they showed an acute perception of what Christianity was really about.

Christianity therefore is about something that happened. It began with something that happened, first, to some women who went to finish off a burial properly and found the body of their Friend gone. It was something that happened, later, to numbers of men and women who had known Jesus previously, when they met Him alive again; in a new form certainly, but quite clearly neither as a ghost nor a vision—phenomena which for them were quite clearly distinguishable from their experience of the risen Christ.

It was what actually happened on Easter Day which only a few weeks later compelled those previously completely disillusioned by the crucifixion and burial of Jesus to go out and convert the world to the new-born creed, 'Christianity.'

The first Christian preaching, described in Acts and the letters of St. Paul and other apostles, is all of a pattern. In the Man Jesus, whom we knew, God has acted in a unique way. Though He was crucified and put to death, God raised up Jesus. In and through Him all men can be completely reconciled with God, a new sort of living has been made

[1]Acts 17.18.

possible. Through the crucified and risen Jesus we call every man everywhere to a radical re-orientation, to a change of heart (repentance), because it is by the crucified and risen Jesus that God will judge the world.

In more modern idiom, Jesus is the yard-stick by which from now on human conduct is to be measured;—the true pattern of human life is at last clear. Yet though a more exacting pattern than any other, God accepts man, God forgives, God imparts a new dynamic, a gracious Presence of Himself by which impossibilities are made possible. All this through the Man Christ Jesus.

Thus everything rests on something quite concrete and quite particular—a Man who died and rose again, and through whose Spirit a new, perfectly concrete and visible community of actual men and women came alive in a new way, gave themselves unsparingly to save others, to be 'for others,' and who had no fear if death were their reward since the Resurrection had finally convinced them that there is in the ultimate Reality of things a Power stronger and more ultimate than death.

Christianity begins then with a Man and something which actually occurred, which was reflected and embodied in the life of an actual community; a group of real men and women who, like the Man, once lived on this earth, and have perpetuated themselves down to our own day because of the reality of their experience and its tangible and visible effects in the life of individuals, and of nations and peoples.

The Man Jesus comes through to us by means of people who have already found Him to be real and alive. They, in their turn, had received this from a previous generation of Christians, and so back through the centuries to Jesus Himself. Here you have a perfectly concrete process of handing on from age to age—an unbroken chain of people who can give evidence that Jesus was alive in their lives, that He meant the supreme thing in their lives, not only as individuals, not only in family life,—but in a community.

Moreover together with the living experience handed on and reproduced—what is in Church language called tradition—there are, to support it and keep it true to itself, writings going back to the age in which Jesus lived—what we know as the New Testament. That which is put down in black and white cannot change. Memory may and does fade. Memory can distort. Tradition also can evolve and proliferate to such a degree that the original impulse from which the tradition starts may become completely subordinated to secondary growths, a phenomenon which is observed in the history and customs of (say) the City of London or the ancient universities; in the significance of uniforms, heraldry etc. Religions of all kinds have always been specially liable to enrich and elaborate their contents at the expense of fidelity to their origins.

But, for the Christian, the New Testament serves not only as a check to false development, but has repeatedly shown itself, surprisingly, to be the source of new insights, as well as the means of recapturing old and important ones covered up by a superabundance of development not strictly harmonious with the original data.

Neither tradition without Scripture, nor Scripture without a living tradition to expound it is in fact adequate. Once the written words are set in isolation from the community which wrote them, which selected them from other writings and through the ages has lived by them, they become not a unifying factor but a source of confusion. Every individual sets his own meaning on the text, especially as the record is often incomplete and assumes so much that is now irrevocably lost.

Nor has the use of scientific historical methods of Bible criticism produced 'the assured results' which were once so confidently claimed for them. To say this is not to make a plea for a return to a pre-critical era, but to realize the limitations of any method which neglects the fundamental fact about both the Old and the New Testaments, that, though the various books contained in them were written by individuals, these individuals were themselves members of communities with a rich common experience and pre-suppositions. Everything is written by 'insiders' and, in the absence of any kind of other evidence, there are no other sources to which we can go. The New Testament was written by Church people for Church people. In the New Testament the Church reflects itself. It is both the mirror, and the object in the mirror.

Above all, of course, Scripture and the Church mirror Christ. It is nearly two thousand years since He walked this earth. There is no life of Him by an outsider—only a few bare facts in non-Christian writings which tell us no more than that He did in fact once exist. Jesus comes to us through the medium of a community and the books which it wrote and passed on to us. There is no other way in which He can come.

Like the Greeks who came to Philip in the Temple, men still demand, 'Sir, we would see Jesus,'[1] and what we offer is a portrait in a mirror—Jesus as reflected in the Bible and in tradition, the living memory of the community of those committed to Him. Reject the mirror or break it up —fragment the New Testament into layers, into strata of various credibility and incredibility, assessed by standards alien to the books themselves; or divide the New Testament

[1]St. John *12*.21.

from the community (the Church) which produced it, and you get, not 'objective truth,' 'real history,' but a mass of subjectivism. *Tot homines quot sententiae*—as many and varied opinions as you have people.

It is true that the Church of Christ is visibly divided (about which more will be said later), but is it divided on the really basic things? Surely not. For the vast majority of Christians still accept the Nicene Creed, and this is all the more remarkable because of their differences of opinion on many other important matters. Now the acceptance of a common Creed is itself, one can see for oneself, something that has happened. In spite of all the division and all the quarrellings, there is still a perfectly concrete recognition of what is fundamental. All gaps in the record apart, there is a *consensus fidelium*, an agreement of the people of God on the ultimate significance of Jesus, His life, death and resurrection, and the Tri-une Nature of God, which breaks through these historical events.

As Archbishop William Temple has said, 'Christianity is the most materialistic of all religions.' It embodies God in a perfectly concrete form, the Man Jesus. It begins with something which happened in time and space, and was seen and handled in flesh and blood. 'The Word was made flesh and dwelt among us.'[1] Christianity is an Event which triggers off a series of events. It is therefore sacramental to the core—a union of visible and invisible—and that is why it is true to real life. There is no thinking without the grey matter of the brain so far as our experience goes. Every word is a vibration which a physicist can measure. Every idea has somewhere in the background a physical image. The very word 'spirit' derives from the sound of our breathing or of the wind, and in language after language we find that

[1] St. John *1*.14.

the word for spirit suggests in rich variety the sound of moving air.

So the Christian Religion was enfleshed in a Man, and has continued in a community of men. Its most sacred rites which the unbroken tradition of the Christian society (and, as the majority hold, Scripture too) ascribes to Jesus Himself, are dependent on material things, namely two of man's most elementary activities, washing in water and eating food. The sacraments are as visible and tangible as the group of men and women who form the Church and the Man Jesus from Whom the Church took its origin. From start to finish Christianity, God's action in Christ, has been 'out there' as everything that is embodied must be. (Bodies exclude one another).

Of course some things 'out there' can become inside one, just as the food I eat which was 'out there' is now in me; but it begins 'out there,' it is originally part of my environment not something deep down inside of me. All the time Jesus comes from outside. He came as a Man who was not any Man but just Himself, not I, not any other. His Church is not I though I can become a member of it. The Scriptures are not I—they too are given. The Sacraments are not I—though I may partake of them.

This objectivity is also demonstrated in episcopacy. It is a commonplace nowadays that the evidence for the shape of the ministry of the Church in the earliest times is incomplete, but *episcope* was *one* of the elements. It finally emerged as the backbone of the visible organization of the Church, and has remained so ever since for the majority of Christians. It is the outward and visible sign of continuity, of discipline and teaching. Thus Scripture, the sacraments of Baptism and Holy Communion, the creeds and historic episcopacy are outward, concrete, objective links with the

Jesus who once lived on this earth, died, rose again and ascended, and lives on through His Spirit in the Church which is His Body and like all bodies is the visible organ through which mind, will, purpose and love function.

But to say all this is not to be blind to the sins and distortions of the Church as a visible society, and in coming later to consider the situation with which the Church has to deal—namely that 'religion-less' society for which Dr. Robinson is so rightly concerned—we ought to take notice first and foremost of the obstacles which the Church itself presents to the acceptance of its own message. We Christians must call ourselves to re-orientation, that is repentance, before we can hope to call others. The very claims we make for Christ and His Church are the measure of our own failure to live out our faith in such concrete, actual forms that they express the truth as it is in Jesus.

Firstly, among the things that hide Christ, must come our divisions—the split between the Orthodox East and the Roman Catholic West—the split between Protestants and Roman Catholics—the continual splitting of Protestants from Protestants. Only in our own day has the tide begun to turn; though in Africa, and elsewhere too, reviving nationalism and the reaction against western paternalism and domination are bearing fruit in further schisms.

Here in our disunity is one cause why men turn their backs on religion. Men long for unity and peace in the world and they see that, in fact, Christians have not even achieved peace among themselves.

It is the contention of this book that however important ways of speaking, of thinking, of presenting Christianity may be, these are not the main reasons why we live in a non-religious age.

Just as there is a massive objectivity about Christ, about Christianity and about the Church, so primarily it is in hard facts, things which are, things which happen *or fail to happen* that the Church fails to communicate to modern man. It is not new words or new images that are desperately needed. We can talk with the tongues of men and of angels (and even of bishops), but if we have not the charity which expresses itself in acts and facts we are nothing. The visible disunity of the Christian Church, the thing Tom, Dick and Harry can see with the naked eye, that *hits* them in the eye, is a major reason why our preaching of Christ in any language, ancient or 'contemporary' has often so little effect.

Secondly there is our history, our past record. Here again an embodied religion, an historical religion, a religion whose Founder gave us the maxim 'by their fruits ye shall know them,'[1] cannot brush off the dark side of its past. We are well aware of the credit side—the transvaluation of values; and more concretely the schools, the hospitals; the humanizing of barbarians in Europe and elsewhere; the countless social advances which have been due to Christians; the part played in the emancipation of the slaves, and so forth.

But as Professor Herbert Butterfield warned us in *Christianity and History*[2] these achievements of Christians can easily be exaggerated. For how long for example did Christians condone slavery? How far are many of our achievements in social justice due to a Christian spirit fostered by the Church, and how far to the organized pressure of the working-classes? Above all, the record of the Church with regard to persecution is one which every Christian

[1] St. Matt, 7.20.
[2] The whole of chapter 7 of this little book should be read in this connection. There is a Fontana paper-back edition of it.

must bewail. From the very moment when the Church itself was freed and received the patronage of the State she herself became a persecutor; and the very ugly story of the cruel persecution of one body of Christians by another in which Protestants, Roman Catholics and Orthodox are all involved, together with the equally shameful persecution of the Jews, make the saddest of all pages of Christian history.

Somehow, therefore, the great scriptural and catholic claims made for the Church and for Christianity as the embodiment (the incarnation) of God's Purpose—for the Church as the Body of the Christ who is Himself the visible Image of invisible Deity—must go side by side with a very clear perception of how the Church, by its divisions and its past record, has often obscured, almost to the point of obliteration, the very things which she exists to manifest in real life. Anyone whose duty it is to expound Scripture Sunday by Sunday, year in and year out, must be painfully aware of the gulf separating his own life and activity, and the life of the Church, from what is said in the same Scripture about Christians as the Body of Christ—Christ's concrete manifestation, the visible sphere in which His life is declared, realized, communicated and extended; where even greater works than those of Christ are to be expected because He has gone to the Father.[1]

Yet we also know that today and all down the ages there are and have been men, women, and children, both as individuals and as groups, who have so let their light so shine before men that their Father in Heaven has been glorified.[2] The practical fruit, which Christ said was the test, has been evident. In the worst days there has always been the real

[1] St. John *14*.12.
[2] St. Matt. *5*.16.

thing. Indeed, if it had not been so, the Church would long ago have perished.

My point is this. The Bishop of Woolwich is very deeply concerned with the 'religion-less' world about him, the people for whom God as a power not ourselves making for justice and goodness, a *deus ex machina* who intervenes, means nothing whatever, or is an incredible bit of out-dated mythology. He is seeking a remedy by trying to find an image of God which such people can accept. He seeks to meet them on their own ground with a God who is not 'outside' but deep-down within.

I would contend that this is not a remedy for the disease but a surrender to it; in fact, a taking of the disease into one's system—falling a victim to it oneself. For Christianity by *its very nature* is something objective, something 'out there' that happened, something embodied in a perfect but actual Human Life and in a visible society of men and women infused by the Spirit of that Life. This is what the New Testament means by Christianity, and this is what Christianity has always meant to Christians ever since. Most certainly it has lost ground, and it is losing ground. (One has only to read for example our modern novels, the 'quality' Sunday papers, the serious weeklies, to see that Christianity is 'out').

Where I disagree totally from Dr. Robinson is in the diagnosis of our condition and, therefore, in its cure. The real snag about Christianity is not in its theories but in its practice. Our present age is far, far too concerned, as it is, with presenting new images;—window-dressing to cover up the inefficiency of too much of our commercial and political life. What Christians need to do is not to think up new images but to deliver the goods! The bishop complains that the Church is too turned in on itself, and his remedy is a century of theological juggling with images!

Where we fail is not in creed but in life; and since Christianity is the religion of God *embodied,* and therefore concerned with *embodying* God in the concrete, in the material, in the actual day to day living, it is to *being and doing* that we must address ourselves, and our thinking must be such as will release Christ and His power.

8

IS 'MAN' ALL THAT 'MATURE'?

WE are told in *Honest to God* that 'man' is now 'come of age,' or to use a hackneyed vogue word, 'mature.' Because 'man' has grown up he must put away kid-stuff, an image of God 'out there,' and find something more adult 'deep down.' (Some, incidentally, with practical experience of the psycho-analyst's divan might question whether 'deep down' is nearer to God,—but let it pass).

However, if Christ is the Image of the invisible God and we as Christians are totally committed to Christ, then there can be no question of a new image. If Christianity is concerned with something that happened, and its basis is something given, then we do not 'look for another.' Jesus Christ is 'He that should come.'[1] That is what Christianity is about.

But let us look at this whole notion of 'man' having 'come of age' and see, if we can, what it demands from those who are to proclaim the Gospel.

To begin with, what is meant by the word 'man'? By 'man' presumably is meant men in general, men as a whole; that is 2,000 million odd of them at the present moment, with a good chance of 3,000 million by the end of the cen-

[1]See St. Matt. *11*.3 ff.

tury, if not before. How can one talk of them in general as being 'mature'?

The trouble about Dr. Robinson and his sophisticated Teutonic mentors is that they create 'man' in their own image, that is the sort of people who not only desire to read all the latest books in their own speciality, but actually have time available to do so by reason of the nature of their jobs (though, of course, Dr. Robinson has recently become a bishop, and this will no doubt limit his ability to keep up with the theological Jones's!).

Of course specialists are absolutely necessary and valuable. The trouble begins when they start generalizing about humanity at large,—'man', in fact.

'Man' at the present moment is a pretty mixed bag. Let us, therefore, drop the rather meaningless abstraction 'man' and take a look at *men* as they actually are. The majority of them are hungry, very poor, illiterate and 'coloured'. Increasingly they are in a ferment, *and rightly so*. They want food, modern industry, education, and proper medical services.

The freedom they want is something perfectly concrete; —freedom to eat, to be able to read, write and have their fair share of the ordinary amenities of life. Reluctantly, the politicians of the 'West' have come to the conclusion that they are not likely to be recruited to fight the battles of 'democracy,' especially if it entails turning their already poverty-stricken countries into radio-active deserts.

Which brings us to another crude fact about 'man' today. One third of the human race lives under communism; and here we have a very active rival both of Christianity and of capitalism.

The communist world cuts across the division between white and coloured races, and also that between east and west. For Marxism was born in Germany and grew to full stature in England in the library of the British Museum. It is a purely western creed in origin, and Russia, where it first triumphed, had a culture which had Graeco-Roman and Christian foundations just as Britain has. Whatever Marxism may be it is therefore not an alien growth. It comes out of the 'West', and is itself a commentary on the meaning of western civilization.

There is no need to develop the point. Generalizations about 'man' at the present time, and for any foreseeable future, are not likely to be true unless they are platitudinous or trivial.

And 'come of age'? Even Dr. Robinson draws attention to the fact that the men who imprisoned and finally killed Bonhoeffer could hardly be called 'mature'. It is a pity he did not pursue this thought a bit further. The men who killed Bonhoeffer, 'liquidated' six million Jews and perpetrated the horrors of Auschwitz and Belsen, were also able to dictate to the most scientific, most cultured, and in many ways the most civilized nation not only in Europe but in the whole world; the nation which produced also the greatest thinkers of modern Protestantism. Moreover, Germany was only freed from Nazi domination by her enemies, among whom the communist-led Russians played a leading role.

Who was 'mature' in all this? And in what sense of the word? If we glance generally round the 'Western' world it becomes more and more baffling to know what 'maturity' means. How 'mature' and 'come of age' are the dictatorships of Spain, Portugal and Turkey, with their grinding poverty and illiteracy, and where revolution is only kept at bay by the harshest methods of repression? How 'mature' is the U.S.A? (By Dr. Robinson's standards the spectacular revival of religion there is linked with just those 'old images' which the 'mature' must get rid of).

And Britain? Recently there was published a really frightening book about this country which has attracted far less attention than it would have done if we were all that 'mature'. The book I am referring to is Anthony Sampson's *Anatomy of Britain*. It is the work of an able and cultured journalist and represents a very solid bit of research. In it every aspect of the forces controlling British life is investigated; the Court, the Cabinet, Parliament, the Civil Service, the Church, the Armed Forces, the Universities, the Law, the City, Big Business of all kinds, the Trades Unions, T.V. and Radio, etc, etc. It is a terrifying picture of *unco-ordinated drift,* in which many even of the people who seem to hold the levers of power are either thwarted by others, or carried along by currents outside their control to goals of which they are only partially aware. Mr. Sampson himself calls his investigation 'a baffling journey,' and the two epigraphs to his last chapter are significant :

' "Everything is always decided *somewhere else"*
(Barbara Wootton)

' "Things fall apart; the centre cannot hold,
Mere anarchy is loosed upon the world."
(W. B. Yeats : *The Second Coming)'*

About twenty lines farther down we read the following :
' "The trouble is," said one Cabinet Minister, "we don't believe in *anything;* we don't believe in Communism, or in anti-Communism, or in free enterprise".'

The statement, therefore, that 'man' has 'come of age' is one without any discoverable meaning, once we begin to look at men 'in the round,' as they actually *are* today, and leave abstractions and generalizations behind.

It might, however, be suggested that what this phrase 'man come of age' means is not 'men in general,' but man in so far as his world is moulded by 'science and technology.' These studies, so we are assured, have made it impossible to believe in a God 'out there'; though, for some reason which is not clear, we are still permitted to believe in a God 'in the depths.'

Now 'science' and 'technology' are wide terms. We are not told which particular science, or what particular department of technology invalidates belief in God. Medicine is usually regarded as a science; but there are numbers of quite orthodox Christian doctors. There have, for example, been *three* Russian bishops recently who started as doctors, one of whom continued to write learned monographs on his medical speciality long after his consecration. Or, again, a top-ranking scientist like Professor C. A. Coulson, with wide knowledge in the fields of quantum theory and theoretical chemistry, finds no difficulty in being a staunch Methodist.

It is, of course, true that each particular science or department of technology is autonomous in the sense that a belief in God does not enter into its experiments or calculations. Everyone knows the old story of the astronomer La Place who, when asked where God came into his theories, replied that he had no need of that hypothesis. But what has the autonomy of particular sciences to do with man's growing-up? The sciences like all other human activities must abstract themselves from the totality of things if they are to make any progress in their chosen sphere. The housewife cannot make a pudding, darn socks and sweep the stairs all at the same time. From the simplest to the most complicated operations of the human hand or brain concentration involving abstraction from what is not relevant to the matter in hand is essential.

A garage mechanic in attempting to locate a fault in your engine would not appear to have reached mental or spiritual maturity because he relies on his technical knowledge and experience to find out what is wrong instead of reciting a decade of the rosary. Nor does one drive a car well through the London rush-hour by meditating upon the perfection of God, however strong one's faith. The autonomy of each science in its own sphere is simply a particular application of a principle which has been with man since civilization began and has got nothing whatever to do with 'growing-up'.

God is not 'edged out of the world' because we understand better how it works. Even if we found out tomorrow how to make life from what is apparently lifeless, it would not affect our belief in God. Men and what they work on with hand or brain are still 'given'. And, even for the purest and most dedicated scientist, there are concretely in his daily life many important things, and above all people, about whom his science may be able to tell him little or, indeed, nothing at all.

As to the applied sciences, it is only too obvious that factors are involved all the time over which each particular science *as such* has no control. From the use or misuse of toxic sprays in agriculture right up to the use or misuse of nuclear fission, it is clear that the question of men's maturity, of their being grown-up, is one of an entirely different order from the purely scientific or technological issues involved. Indeed one might say that the more specialized science becomes and the less specialists, even in different branches of the same science, are able fully to communicate with one another, the less possible will it be to say, from a purely scientific standpoint, that God has been edged out of the world as a whole.

The real reasons why God and religion are, in Britain and many other countries, being brushed aside are, I believe, of a much more concrete and specific nature than Man's mythological maturity, and his supposed dissatisfaction with the imagery of God; and some of these reasons we shall now go on to consider. But before we do this a warning needs to be uttered.

Does it automatically follow, for example, that because only 10 per cent of our population in England are regular worshippers, that therefore the fault lies with the churches' faith? This would seem from the Gospels to be a quite gratuitous assumption. Indeed, it may very well be that if Christ were proclaimed more effectively the churches might be emptier still! As Dean Inge observed, the big battalions are not drawn up outside the narrow way. 'The customer is always right' may be a good business slogan, but it is quite fatal in the Church. The basic problem of communication is not *how* we put things but *what* we put. Yet 'Turn it upside down or inside out and perhaps Jones will swallow it after all' seems to be an attitude nowadays which is all too widespread. May it not be that it is our popularity rather than our unpopularity that should most worry us? The Gospels are full of the theme that servants must not expect to get better treatment than their Master—and the Master was rejected and crucified.

Of course, this could be a high-sounding rationalization of quite inexcusable failures and Scripture itself tells us of offences which are certainly not 'the offence of the Cross.'[1] Nevertheless, before any discussion of the great recession in religion, it is well to remind ourselves of what the New Testament has to say about the reception accorded to Him,

[1] For example St. Matt. *18*.7.

who is after all, if Christianity be true, the Way, the Truth and the Life.

What pushes God out of many people's lives is just the experiences of life itself. I have said that Christianity is primarily about something which happened. Unbelief, rejection of Christianity, is also about something which has happened or *failed to happen*.

There is, for example, nothing very mysterious (in general terms) about why the working classes of Britain were lost to the Church. The harshness of the industrial revolution and the slums, with the paucity of churches during the formative period, saw to that. Two world-wars, 'the Bomb', and the frightful instability of the international situation generally, have done for the middle classes what the industrial revolution did for the workers. The appalling amount of mental illness, the suicides and—what few people unfamiliar with the inside of hospitals realize—the *attempted* suicides, all point in the same direction.

The affluence which has now (rightly) come to the majority of British working people is overshadowed by the knowledge that a few H-bombs would mean goodbye too all that! A grammar-school boy recently asked what he would do when he left school, replied 'what's the good of thinking about *that* when probably I shan't be here?' It is the sheer meaningless of life under the threat of nuclear extinction that goes far to explain the 'inexplicable' conduct of a minority of young people who have to live in the madhouse created by man 'come of age'. But the majority of all ages, and in all classes, prefer not to think about the realities of nuclear warfare; and the psychologists have taught us what happens when we push realities to the back of our minds. Never has security been so much talked about, and never was the human race less secure.

Is there anything peculiarly recondite in the question why people no longer believe in a loving heavenly Father either 'up there' or 'out there'—or even 'down there'? The fact is that there are far, far, too many who have either known personally the barbarities of war and revolution, or who have friends and near relations who have been 'through it'. No wonder Bonhoeffer in his cell, awaiting certain death, after witnessing for ten years the Nazi enslavement of the German people, could speak of a God who allows Himself 'to be edged out of the world onto the Cross'! Yet Bonhoeffer never lost his faith, though I think we do him a grave injustice when we try to weave a new doctrine out of the strange fragmentary utterances in which he tried to ex-express that faith to his friend.

Moreover, in addition to the general situations in which men find themselves today, there are those things in personal life which have always tested faith; the inexplicable tragedies and injustices, the suffering of innocent people, especially of children; the seeming uselessness of prayer, and so forth.

It is, I repeat, surely life itself that makes against belief in most cases. It is the contradiction in real life between any image of God as good, whether God is 'above,' 'beneath' or 'within,' that makes men atheists. Yet how few books and how few sermons touch on this basic problem! Our theological libraries are crammed with books devoted to every aspect of textual and higher criticism of the Bible, but of genuine theological thinking about the things which drive religion from men's hearts there is appallingly little to be found. The archaeology of Christian origins seems largely to have replaced genuine theology.

The fact is that belief in a good God is impossible to anyone who looks at life as it really is, unless they are prepared to take Christ as their Image of God. 'No man cometh unto the Father but by Me'[1] enunciates a fundamental truth. Without the Image of the crucified and risen Christ, God as Father is literally invisible. You don't see Him, you *can't* see Him. God is certainly 'edged out of the world onto the Cross'— the Cross of the ideal good coming to the ideally bad end; the sheer powerlessness of God in comparison with the brute force of 'the powers that be'.

But the Cross by itself would be no Gospel—no *good* news whatsoever, only one more piece of badness—unless the same Christ-Image of God really and truly rose from the dead and became 'the first fruits of them that slept'.[2] This is why 'there is none other Name given under Heaven whereby we must be saved'.[3] This is not a bit of Christian pride and exclusiveness. This is just rock-bottom reality. Both the death of the innocent Christ, that is the crushing of Christ by that which governs this world, *and* the resurrection of Christ (by death defeating death) are essential if we are to believe in God at all. Here you can see what is otherwise invisible. Our failure in proclaiming Christianity has not been a failure to have up-to-date images. On the contrary, it has been a failure to make the oldest images in our faith—the Cross and the Resurrection, real and sharply-defined. And this, I believe, is due to our desire to make Christianity the cement of society instead of the leaven in the lump.

As Albert Schweitzer remarked long ago, 'the world affirms itself automatically'.[4] It does not need Christianity to do what it can well do on its own. The Christian task is a very different one.

[1] St. John *14*.6.
[2] I Corinthians *15*.20.
[3] Acts *4*.12.
[4] *The Quest of the Historical Jesus*, p. 400.

4

9

CHRIST IS RISEN

I have been saying that I believe that it is the experience of evil and suffering which is the main reason for the decay of religious faith. The old dilemma with which St Augustine wrestled is with us more vividly than ever before. As paraphrased by C. E. M. Joad—'Either God cannot abolish evil or He will not. If He cannot He is not omnipotent; if He will not He is not benevolent'.[1]

Many religious philosophers have attempted at one time or another to illuminate this problem. Clearly it would be impossible to go over the ground again here. Leibniz thought he had produced the perfect answer over 250 years ago; but it would satisfy few people today and is, in any case, far too difficult and lengthy a work for any but theologians and philosophers to read. The verdict of theologians of the last generation like Dr N. P. Williams or Dean Inge was that the problem of evil is 'probably insoluble'—that is on the purely theoretical plane.

A mystical thinker like Jakob Boehme and a modern religious philosopher like Nicolas Berdyaev (who was deeply

[1]The story of Joad's conversion to Christianity after a life-time of agnosticism and his return to the Church of England is a very striking one. *The Recovery of Belief*, C. E. M. Joad. (Faber & Faber).

influenced by Boehme) are certainly right in connecting the problem of evil with the existence of real freedom in man. Without freedom man is not man at all, but a mere puppet in the hands of his Creator or whatever force brought man into existence. But real freedom means the possibility of evil as well as good, of hatred and cruelty as well as of 'love, joy and peace'.

Men complain bitterly of the cruelty and injustice of life; the terrors of war, anarchy and the prospect of a sub-human existence in a radio-active desert for their descendants, the 'survivors' of nuclear war. But, while not forgetting the cruelties of Nature 'red in tooth and claw', it has to be admitted that most of the things which make life beastly are man-made or man-tolerated. The sciences, for example, if properly used, could abolish an incredible amount of human suffering in the way of hunger and disease. But scientists like other people can only do the work the community at large is prepared to pay for; and as theirs is a particularly costly work in terms of finance, they are perhaps more dependent on what the public thinks it wants than many others.

In a word 'man's greatest enemy is "man" and "man" is precisely *not* "come of age" nor "mature".'

Now the contemporary situation is not only man's cross; —it is what David Edwards rightly called *God's Cross in our world*. Christ crucified as the Image of the invisible God —the God blacked out by all the evil, particularly the senseless and wanton evil, of life—is here our only Saviour, the One who is 'in it' with each one of us, but who has also risen from the dead and ever lives.

But the death of Christ was not an accident, a miscalculation of the political and ecclesiastical forces arrayed against Him in Jerusalem. *'No man taketh my life from me,*

I lay it down.[1] And this laying down of life was His supreme act 'for others'. He called it a 'ransom'[2]—that is, a liberating act;—it freed men from everything that gets between them and God, and therefore from much more than sin; such things as the oppressive sense of the meaninglessness of life, of fear before life's evils, of insecurity and its blind cruelty.

The trouble is that the Cross has often been preached in too narrow terms. For example 'bearing the Cross' has been restricted too much to putting-up bravely with the troubles of everyday life. It is of course that, but that is only part of the truth. Or, again, sickness is spoken of as a cross, which in turn has led to an idea not found anywhere in the Gospels that 'God sends sickness to try us'. (On the contrary, sickness, like sin, was something to which Christ always took an aggressive attitude. These were things to be eliminated from God's world). In general, passages glorifying suffering in the New Testament have too often been wrenched from their context. Take for example the service for *The Visitation of the Sick*. Here Hebrews *12*.5 and 6 is quoted in which it is said that the Lord loves those whom he chastens and scourges, every son whom He receives. Now the context makes it quite clear that the sufferings mentioned are not those of sickness but those caused by persecution for fidelity to Christ.

There is no glorification of suffering for its own sake, no cult of suffering, in the New Testament. Rather suffering is glorious because it sets a seal on real committal to Christ. As we are identified realistically and unreservedly with Him and His cause so we must expect to suffer, because 'a servant is not greater than his lord'.[3] Sickness, on the other

[1] St. John *10*.18.
[2] St. Mark *10*.45.
[3] St. John *13*.16.

hand, in the New Testament is something to be healed;—though if it cannot be healed it is to be used to unite us to God, as Christians all down the ages have agreed.

There is another way, too, in which the preaching of the Cross is often inadequate. The Cross has to be seen also as a symbol of conflict, especially with the ruling powers of 'this world'. The very shape of the Cross is a pattern of conflict—the vertical cutting across the horizontal. It is therefore a mistake to regard the Cross as something purely passive. Jesus went up to Jerusalem to throw down a challenge, both to Church and State; and the result was, as He clearly foresaw, the Cross. Jesus spoke of His followers *taking up* the Cross, which meant literally taking up part of the scaffold (as it were) upon which you were to be put to death by respectable society, by constituted authority. The Cross, in other words, has a revolutionary significance. It represents a programme of life so radical and obnoxious to the established order as to result in crucifixion. *The Passion of Christ was in fact the Action of Christ.*

Above all, the Passion and Crucifixion of Jesus Christ the God-Man is not only something which once happened far away and long ago. It is not just a Man who suffers and dies though innocent; it is the Passion of Man and God. 'God was in Christ reconciling the world unto Himself'.[1] For man often feels like Fitzgerald's Omar :

'For all the sin wherewith the face of man is blackened,
    Man's forgiveness give—and take !'

Men are often unreconciled to God who, in their dark and bitter moments, they feel has trapped them into an existence into which they did not ask to be born. The acids of daily life and of our terrible world-situation bite into men. Men cry out against a God who can do nothing about

[1] II Corinthians 5.19.

it—against the *Deus* who is, after all, not *ex machina;* the God who doesn't help 'from outside', and to whom men in their agony pray in vain.

What is the evidence they ask for such a God who can help? Where do we see Him at work in real life? The nation-states and their hideous armaments devouring even in 'peace' the resources that could feed the hungry; the ever-growing and ever more impersonal structure of industrial and commercial life; the vast forces of nationalism and racialism—what do all these care for the individual human life as they grind on their way? Yes; men *are* unreconciled to a God who brought all this into being, and who now appears to look on helplessly.

The first Good Friday evening, for anyone who had known and loved Jesus, brought just such a feeling of despair and disillusionment. For had not Jesus' Gethsemane prayer that the Cup of suffering might pass been, to human understanding, refused? Above all, had not Jesus Himself cried out on the Cross 'My God, My God, why hast thou forsaken me?'[1] The story of Jesus, then, had it really finished with His burial, would have been a perfect theme for yet another Thomas Hardy novel. If ever God should have intervened to save a righteous man Good Friday was the Day. But no one—not Elias, nor anyone, came to take Jesus off the cross until He was dead, so far as this earth and this life were concerned.

No wonder, therefore, that St. Paul wrote about the 'weakness and foolishness' of God![2] We, as Christian preachers, have not made nearly enough of this, and so have failed to bring it home in everyday language to ordinary men and women. God in Jesus *has* plumbed human

[1] St. Mark *15*.34.
[2] I Corinthians *1*.25.

misery to the bottom. Mental, spiritual and physical suffering; even paradoxically God-forsakenness; the bitter mocking of clever people and 'The Establishment'; failure, disgrace, betrayal, desertion; the whole gamut, until death itself arrived.

Nevertheless, 'the foolishness of God is wiser than men, and the weakness of God (what is weaker than an expiring, tortured, nailed-down body?) is stronger than men'.[1]

The philosophers are right. There is no logical or theoretical answer to the problems of evil. The very origin of evil remains a mystery.

The Christian 'answer' is, again, something that happened. It points to a good Man, in whose mouth was no guile, crucified, dead and buried, but *risen again,* and says 'Behold your God!'.

Yet have we in practice given to the Resurrection of the crucified God-Man its central importance? In particular has Western Christianity done this? Look, for example, at our church buildings. The crucifix, the cross with the dying or the dead Christ is to be seen everywhere. In Lutheran churches, when other images were removed, it became specially prominent. In Anglican churches the crucifixion is the favourite subject for an east window. In the Anglican consecration prayer in the Eucharist only the Cross and Passion of Christ are recalled. In Roman Catholic churches the Stations of the Cross are very much in evidence. All this is right: but where is the Resurrection portrayed? There is surely nothing accidental in all this. (By contrast however, in the churches of the Orthodox East, the ikon of the crucifixion very often has to be looked for, and it is the Resurrection or Christ as *Pantocrator* which is the focus of the east end, though hidden by the screen).

[1] *Ibid.*

Yet without the story of Easter Day, Good Friday is incomplete. True our Lord said 'I, if I be lifted up from the earth will draw all men unto me'.[1] True also (as Archbishop William Temple loved to remind us) that it is as Christ ascends to the Cross that He is glorified. The glory is in the self-giving love. Nevertheless, 'if Christ be not risen then is our preaching vain'.[2] For the glory of the Cross, of the perfect sacrificial love, was only made apparent on Easter Day. We cannot separate Calvary from the Empty Tomb, and the appearances of the risen Christ. That is why the Resurrection dominates the first preaching of the Apostles. Can it honestly be said that it has dominated ours?

But once again the proportion of the Faith is needed. The wonder and glory of Easter are not exhausted by the demonstration that death is not the end; though that in itself is such an overwhelming, tremendous, releasing and joyous thing, and such a powerful source of comfort and good cheer. Not even the vindication of our Lord Himself is the whole story. There is intertwined with these, the most important elements in the Easter message, another truth particularly needed today. God's Easter Victory was worked out, as it were, on another 'plane'.

The sequel to the story of Jesus Christ, the very thing that makes it relevant to man's desperate need in a world where goodness is crucified, belongs to the supernatural.

The last movement of earth's symphony will therefore also be in another key. It is in the light of the Resurrection of Christ that we look to the future both of ourselves and of humanity.

Just as Christianity is rooted in something which has

[1] St. John 12.32.
[2] I Corinthians 15.14.

happened, so it looks forward to something which will happen, but in another dimension. Life on earth is not self-explanatory. To put it another way, the centre of gravity is revealed by the Resurrection to be outside space and time. Christians cannot therefore claim that their Faith is justified in terms of space, time, or within the history either of the human race or of individuals. Christianity frankly calls a new world into being to redress the balance of the old.

This is a truth that can only be accepted by faith. No evidence from ancient documents can be compelling, in the nature of the case, because the writers are dead. They cannot now be cross-examined, and of the hostile witnesses no record remains at all. But though the evidence cannot coerce, it is there;—some of it going back, even in its present form, to only twenty years after the event. It is evidence which can be reasonably accepted for the very reason that it does not stand alone. The religion built on the Resurrection is still with us. It has commanded the allegiance of many of the worlds cleverest men and deepest thinkers as well as of the very simplest souls.

Men, women and children of every race and every culture have accepted the Faith of Christ crucified and risen again. They have lived by it; it has been the most real thing in their lives. They have also died in it, and often for it. As someone once put it, 'I believe witnesses who are prepared to die for their evidence'. So, too, on every first day of the week since those early days, Christians have met together to break the bread and drink the cup; to set forth before God and man the victorious death of the Carpenter of Nazareth. Thus the evidence is not only the Man Jesus and the records of His life, death and Resurrection; there is also the living chain of men and women all down the ages who have lived and are living in the power of His endless life.

The Christian community, the Church, is built on apostles and prophets—men and women who believe and have believed; though of course 'the chief corner-stone' is Christ Himself.[1] This is something beyond nature, and it points to what is beyond nature, as the ultimate goal of mankind and of his world. In this faith men can face with God Himself the crucifixion of goodness, which is the greatest destroyer of faith, confident that by death God has destroyed death and that the last word is with Life.

[1]Ephesians 2.20.

10

FREEDOM IN CHRIST

IN a striking passage in one of his works (unfortunately still untranslated) V. Rosanov complains bitterly that Christians have made so little *creative* use of the freedom brought them by Christ.

The real meaning and significance of Calvary, he says, are generally misunderstood. 'The Saviour died—man was raised from the dead. Christ descended into hell—man came out of hell. God goes to man's prison . . . What then does man the prisoner do? Man goes back to prison. God I will be with Thee! Such is the thousand-year-old logic of Christianity! God entered the prison-house, was bound and spat upon, wore the crown of thorns, precisely in order that man might no longer be confined, but might escape.

Yet it is as if man failed to comprehend what had happened to him, or even denied that it happened at all; and so he remains immobile in prison. Such action might seem at first sight to be religious, but in essence it is blasphemous . . . The work of Jesus, the whole act of redemption, has somehow by-passed man: man has fallen into a kind of abyss. Somehow we have failed to *notice* our liberation. Here lies the origin of all Christian pessimism—a pessimism which very often approximates to that of Schopenhauer himself!'[1]

'I came,' said Christ, 'that they might have life and have it more abundantly'.[2] How right, therefore, is the Bishop of Woolwich when he says that the Church must be outward-looking! For the new life brought to man by Christ's Death and Resurrection is meant to flow out through Christians into the whole wide world. That is precisely why they are baptized into Christ; to be members of His Body,— lips, hands, feet which He can use for the service of the world. For Christians like their Master come not to be served, but to serve others. That is their job : *that is what they are for.*

But as the late Pope John reminded us in his encyclical *Pacem in terris* this going out into the world on the part of ordinary Christians, 'the lay apostolate' as our Roman brethren call it, demands expert knowledge. 'In order to imbue civilization with sound principles and enliven it with the spirit of the gospel, it is not enough to be illumined with the gift of Faith and enkindled with the desire of forwarding a good cause. For this end it is necessary to take an active part in the various organizations and influence them from within. And since our present age is one of outstanding scientific and technical progress and excellence, one will not be able to enter these organizations and work effectively from within unless he is scientifically competent, technically capable and skilled in the practice of his own profession.'

Technical competence, expertize, however, is not enough : 'Faith', as the Pope goes on to say, 'should be present as a beacon to give light, Charity as a force to give life'.[3]

---

[1]V. V. Rosanov *Okolo Tserkovnykh sten.* A copy of this two volume work exists in the British Museum Library. It was written some 55 years ago.
[2]St. John *10.*10.
[3]*Pacem in terris* p. 39. (English translation).

It is here that we encounter the *trahison des clercs* and, in particular, *des théologiens*. Theology in general, instead of acting as a beacon-light to guide the people of God, the laity, as they confront the problems of living for Christ in the world, has for generations been taking refuge in an ever more and more minute study of Christian origins. Theology is less and less about God and God's world and more and more a department of ancient history absorbed in minute details of historical and literary criticism. The whole business is wildly out of proportion.

Our modern theologians are in danger of becoming nothing but historians and archaeologists, concerned simply with the past. While one cannot be too grateful for much that 150 years of biblical criticism has achieved the movement is quite obviously running to seed.

A recent article by Dr Alec Vidler in *The Sunday Times* was extremely interesting and refreshing in this connection. It was one of a series dealing with the position of the arts faculties in the universities today—literature, history, classics, etc. In each of these articles there was the same healthy protest against the dry-as-dust, 'inhuman' and remote way in which the so-called 'humanities' are increasingly expounded. That these protests have come from the heart of the universities (and even the ancient universities) is a hopeful feature in an otherwise dismal prospect.

Theology, of course, was once the queen of sciences; but she misused her position to dictate to other disciplines and branches of learning both their methods and their conclusions. A revolt therefore was both inevitable and just.

But this is no reason why theology must abdicate her duty to see life as a whole with the light of God and to relate other disciplines and sciences to those divinely given truths on which the Christian Church is founded. If the ordinary Christian is to live creatively and to shed the light of Faith, both on the problems of each particular sphere of activity and also on the present historical situation in which we all are involved, then theologians have a tremendous task ahead of them and a grave responsibility.

What is needed today is far less concern with archaeological hair-splitting, and far more restraint in the exercise of pure imagination on those matters where the scarcity of verifiable facts makes certainty impossible. Together with this must go a great deal more hard thinking about the world as it is, what we as Christians have to do in it, and whither Christ's spirit is leading us.

This is one more reason why *Honest to God* is such a deplorable piece of work. It laments the self-absorption of the Church only to provide her with more fodder for ingrowing speculation, instead of holding up the already given light of Christ, the Image of God, to a distracted, floundering civilization.

For western civilization is certainly adrift. Once it professed and called itself Christian and, though it often failed to live up to its profession, at least it possessed generally-recognized standards by which it could criticize itself. Christianity, as a mere matter of history, has certainly played a big part in moulding western civilization. Today, however, it is usual to speak of our age as the *post*-Christian era.

Most of us, indeed, find abundant confirmation of the accuracy of this description in our daily lives. But if anyone doubts it, our novels, our newspapers (especially the Sunday ones), T.V., the theatre, etc., provide ample corroboration of the fact that Christianity is a back number—outdated.

There is much also in music and the plastic arts which reflect (as art cannot help reflecting, however loudly it may proclaim the doctrine of art for art's sake) the authentic quality of contemporary life as undefined, uncommitted, adrift. Whether one likes or dislikes abstract art it is in any case a portent.

Another feature of life today, revealing its divergence from Christianity and its rootlessness, is our obsession with sex and its deliberate exploitation for purely commercial ends. While the fact that sex can be so freely and openly discussed is a great gain, it is also extremely tedious that one can so rarely escape from it, and that it is all so appallingly self-conscious. What our advertisers would do without it is a real problem ! As to our literature, Dean Inge was complaining forty years ago of 'a generation which will not buy a novel unless it contains some scabrous story of adultery'. Today we have got far beyond that in the detailed description of all the preliminaries of the sex act, even when that itself is not described.

This sort of thing may, of course, in the end work its own cure. Somerset Maugham is reported to have said that after reading seventy pages of *Lolita* he could read no more, as it bored him so dreadfully; and a healthy young farmer I know had a very similar thing to say about the unexpurgated version of *Lady Chatterley's Lover*. Though no Puritan himself, he added that he felt England was about due for a Puritan reaction—and so it may be . . . Anyhow the point is that our present obsession with sex is certainly mirrored in the novel, and of course further stimulated by it, as is also the rejection of any kind of Christian standards in the matter.

Whether there is a great deal more sexual promiscuity than there was is very difficult to say as, in the nature of the case, no statistics are available; but what is quite certain is that promiscuity is a much more *obvious* feature of our life, that it excites far, far less criticism, and that chastity, or virginity, is now on the defensive in many circles. It is also true that the invention of reliable contraceptives has made it much more possible for boys and girls from respectable homes to sit loosely to Christian moral standards. The figures for venereal disease are also very disquieting.

The young are much criticized nowadays, but it is their elders who are most to be condemned; for it is older people who are entirely responsible for the whole gamut of money-making sex exploitation from the expensive strip-tease joints (most patronized by those past fifty) to the cheap pornography of the 'surgical goods' shops in our streets with schoolboys, on their way home, glueing their eyes to the windows. The whole business is a disgusting betrayal of youth, and could be stopped overnight if our 'free society' had the will to use its 'freedom' for decent ends.[1]

The police in this and other matters (details of which my readers may be spared) are hamstrung by our inadequate laws. Yet as soon as it is suggested that the law might be tightened up, at once we have the parrot-cry that liberty is in danger. Am I exaggerating? 'English audiences are probably unaware that they have the reputation for being the dirtiest minded in Europe', observes Harold Hobson the theatre critic in a recent issue of the *Sunday Times*; and though he thinks this a misconception, he admits that there *are* moments when his confidence is shaken.

If we were not traditionally so impervious to foreigners' criticisms (almost the sole characteristic which we still share with the despised Victorians!) we might be seriously worried by what some overseas visitors (from Billy Graham at the one end of the ideological spectrum to Russian or Chinese communists at the other) have to say about such things as

---

[1] Twice recently there have been reports in the national press of teenagers' organizing protests against commercial exploitation of sex.

our sex behaviour in public. Indeed only the blind, the sentimental or the complacent can fail to observe from their daily experience as well as from what they read that we are living in an age of extremely loose sexual standards. And this is a well-known characteristic of a civilization that is drifting.

The ethical 'woolliness' of Dr Robinson, like that to be found in *Soundings*, is untrue to the New Testament, and completely useless to those who are already only too painfully aware of the lack of standards about them and the temptation to drift with the crowd.

The fact is that sex only falls into its natural place in the scale of any man's activities when a man knows what life in general is for, and when he lives in a society which has some purpose beyond that of keeping itself going and patting itself on the back because it has 'never had it so good'. The Christian, while having a positive attitude towards sex as part of his God-given make-up, knows also that life is more than the satisfaction of sex, hunger and thirst. Therefore to give sex the inflated significance which it has today is to divert energy and attention from even more significant and valuable ends. A glutton who lives to eat is rightly censured as one who mistakes the means of life for the end.

The sex obsession built up artificially today is, I repeat, an indication that our civilization is drifting, and that it has no really worth-while aim or satisfying purpose. Thus sex is degraded from its lofty intention to serve as a mere diversion, a means of titillation for people who are frustrated by the cheap, fragmentary character of the life surrounding them.

But 'post-Christian' is inadequate as a description of our age. It merely registers the historical fact that being committed to Christ and His way of life is now the concern of only a small minority. But if most men are not for Christ, what are they for?

The answer normally given is that we have no dominant ideology, that we are a 'plural' society or a 'free' society. Both of these terms recall the story of the emperor's clothes. A certain emperor, a prisoner of flattery like many of his ilk, paraded before his subjects in what was given out to be the most superb and finely-woven garment ever made. The whole show was indeed remarkably impressive until a rude little boy was bold enough to remark that in actual fact the emperor was stark naked.

The words 'plural society' are a meaningless phrase designed to conceal the true nakedness of the land,—the plain fact that we have lost any common worth-while purpose. The term 'free society' is equally pompous nonsense, for, unless it is defined what one is free *for,* it would apply equally well to an assortment of white mice let out of their cage on to a Victorian nursery floor.

Why not be honest to God and honest to man, and admit that we are clue-less; pursuing our own ends, each with our own scale of values, with such cohesion as derives merely from convenience or necessity. Few people seem to be aware of the wide variety of senses in which the word freedom can be used, or of the various strata of freedom so penetratingly analysed and described for instance in such books as Berdyaev's *Freedom and the Spirit.*

Not only is freedom a word of many meanings in itself, but however interpreted it requires that we ask 'freedom *from* what, freedom *for* whom, and freedom *for* what?' During the first world-war, for example, statements that we were fighting for freedom certainly had a very precise *negative* connotation which united the vast mass of our people. However much we differed among ourselves we were quite clear that we did *not* want to be ruled by the Kaiser. But the industrial troubles of the twenties, and later the great depression, showed very clearly that the questions, freedom 'for whom?' and 'for what?' had not been answered. The old jibe that any Britisher is 'free' to dine at the Ritz, after all, still contains a deep truth. Anyone is 'free' to open a small shop in Britain, and is equally 'free' to be put into the gutter by a new chain-store or supermarket in 'free' competition with him . . . and so on through many other levels of our life.

But by the far most alarming feature of all this complacent 'conformist' meaningless chatter about a 'free' society, is that we are surrounded today by an increasing number of our fellowmen who know collectively very well what they want and what they stand for. While we drift, allowing our course to be set (when it is set) by a temporarily achieved equilibrium between competing internal pressures, there are others who are aware of some very clear directives.

It is often said that we live in an age of rapid revolutionary change, but practical conclusions are not being drawn from this observation. We live by improvization. We no longer direct; we react, we tinker with things. And the general principle seems to be, 'for heaven's sake leave things alone wherever possible—legislate, plan ahead as little as may be' (though now, with our failure to get into the Common Market, it looks as if at least in the economic sphere we may try to look farther than the end of our noses!).

But in the big world outside most men know where they are going or where they want to go, not till the next general election, but perhaps for centuries.

There is firstly the hungry, poor, illiterate majority of the human race. Increasingly these people are determined to put up with their miseries no longer. The privileged nations are helping—but are they helping enough and fast enough? We might spare some of the excessive attention now devoted to sex and reflect that biologically nutrition is an even more fundamental drive than sex! More and more the hungry know that they need not be hungry if the technical resources of the world were developed for their benefit instead of being channelled so lavishly into preparations for a world holocaust.

One of the very best things therefore that the churches are doing is Inter-Church Aid for the hungry. Not that private charity can finally solve the problem, but because, while helping some, it bears witness to Christ and stirs the conscience of western civilization to turn from dead works to serve the living God, and *therefore man His creature*. Here again we must remember that freedom to eat, freedom from preventible diseases and freedom to make use of modern technology are infinitely more real to half the world's population than freedom for 'the western way of life,' in 'defence' of which some of us are prepared to blow to pieces both ourselves and the bulk of humanity.

11

FOR CHRIST'S SAKE

CLOSELY tied up with the purpose of the hungry and illiterate to achieve a better life is the whole problem of race, for the under-privileged are for the most part also the 'coloured'.

Africans and Asians, who far outnumber Europeans and their descendants in the U.S.A. and the Commonwealth, are no longer going to be content with a back seat. One need not labour this point. Ours is a predominantly 'coloured' world and mastery of technology which has been the basis of the white man's ascendancy is more and more rapidly being acquired by Africans and Asians.

'The shape of things to come' could not be clearer, and if the opportunity of partnership between the races were firmly grasped now the whole world would be richer and happier for it. Yet here in Britain, for example, in the name of 'freedom', nothing must be done to deal *effectively* with incitement to race-hatred and our unofficial but quite real colour-bar. Madame Roland's famous last words on the steps of the guillotine about liberty are only too relevant to modern Britain.

A third feature of the big world in which our 'plural' society is drifting about is communism. I have mentioned this before, but more needs to be said about it here. With a third of the world's inhabitants living under communist régimes, and with communist or near-communist parties in almost every land, the matter cannot be ignored. There are those in Britain who hate communism sufficiently to talk about it incessantly, and there are also those who cordially approve—and also constantly speak about it. But in between these two extremes lies the great mass of our people, including nearly all church people, who prefer to remain silent; who are afraid even to discuss the subject 'because it is so controversial'.

This is a quite ridiculous state of affairs. We simply cannot ignore one of the greatest forces moulding the future. How many people know, for example, that a few years ago UNESCO reported that there were more translations of Lenin than of the Bible? How many people realize that the largest parties both in France and Italy are communist?

Communists certainly know what they want and are willing to make tremendous sacrifices to achieve it. I knew a Russian lawyer, who eventually settled in Britain, who had worked for years with the communists, knowing personally many of their top people. He never ceased to be staggered by the capacity of these men for iron self-discipline and prodigious hard work. It is precisely this dedicated spirit and capacity for self-sacrifice which has been a major factor in the long series of communist successes.

Behind the whole movement, as we know, is the philosophy of dialectical materialism which in its all-embracing scope can only be compared with religion. Every aspect of life is related to this central creed. It is all very well British intellectuals sneering at Marxism as out-of-date stuff, but it is after all what makes two of the three largest nations in the world 'tick'. Moreover, Marxism is something which, for all its elaboration, can be presented in extremely simple terms even to illiterate people.

'It is your work that creates wealth', says the communist to the poor and hungry labourer, 'but you are not getting your fair share. However, the bosses' world is cracking up as anything based on individual self-interest *must* do sooner or later. Every society divided into "haves" and "have-nots" has perished from the conflicts it has itself created. You need no God "outside"; the forces of real life itself are creating the conditions for a new, just, reasonable and moral order of society. All you have to do is to play your part under the leadership of the communists who have the scientific knowledge necessary to make the successful change'.

Our cold-war propaganda has been quite disastrous. It stems from the days when America alone had the A-bomb, and it was believed that communism could be blotted out for ever in one devastating blow. And to justify such wholesale massacre communism had to be represented as something even more evil than Hitlerism. Now that Russia has both the A and the H bombs, with the practical certainty that China will not lag far behind, the situation is quite different. If we are not prepared to live with communism the only alternative is the suicide of nuclear war. Yet if we are going to live with communism we can only do so on a basis of truth and reality. That is common-sense and it is also Christian sense.

Most British people—as one knows from lecturing on the subject—are (thanks to our cold-war propaganda) amazingly unaware of some of the most elementary facts about Russia. They have, for example, little conception of the appalling and hideous conditions of life under the tsars; of the people's illiteracy; of the frightful housing conditions; of the constant famines and the chronic undernourishment of the majority of the population; in a word, of all the things which made revolution inevitable. What the Soviet rule has done in about 45 years, in spite of the German invasion (which among other things left twenty million people homeless), is one of the most staggering achievements in the whole of recorded history.

In education, in science and technology, in health, in the housing, clothing and feeding of the people, and in industry the progress made is quite fantastic. The dynamism can be felt. True, there are still a number of things not up to standards achieved by some western European nations who have behind them a far longer history of industrial development. But this is a trifling criticism. Clearly, from what has already been achieved, deficiencies can soon be made good when more important things have been dealt with.

What escapes the British and American observer is that the most significant thing is not how Russia appears to *us*, but how it looks to the great majority of the world's inhabitants who are hungry, poor and industrially and educationally backward. Anyone who has lived and worked in Asia or Africa and known their hideous poverty and their longing for radical change will see the point. For while we think of what we should *lose* if England went communist, more than half the world is calculating daily what it might perhaps *gain* if it took a leaf out of Russia's or China's book.

Let us take a new look at communism from the angle of world poverty, which, as I have said, is the crucial angle from which to regard humanity today. For our own industrial and commercial life is geared to dividends. People put their money where it can earn most with greatest security. Is a system where money rules in this way able to finance the rehabilitation of a hungry world? Or will this not rather be done by those who put human need first, and who are therefore prepared to conscript land, wealth and labour for the common good? Once more, the important thing is not how affluent Britons in their plural society answer this question, but how the hungry, illiterate and coloured majority of humanity will answer it. And it is on *their* answer that the future history of our planet will be decided —*not ours*.

We have dwelt too long upon the errors of communism, its atheism and the crimes of certain communists, forgetting, among other things, much in the history of other countries— our own included—which has over the centuries also deserved severe condemnation. It is time that Christians at any rate took a more truthful and a more objective line, recognizing that it is the virtues and not the vices of communism which are responsible for its very solid achievements.

It is the virtues of communism too which exercise a tremendously attractive power on all who want to improve the lot of their peoples and give them a reasonably decent standard of living and of culture. The Pope, therefore, gave a splendid lead when he wrote (obviously with communism in mind) 'Who can deny that those movements, in so far as they conform to the dictates of right reason and are interpreters of the lawful aspirations of the human person, contain elements that are positive and *deserving of approval*?'[1]

Overshadowing everything in our contemporary situation there is the menace of nuclear war. Everyone knows that an all-out nuclear war means suicide. It has been said, for example, by men like Mr Eisenhower and Lord Home,

[1]*Pacem in terris* p. 41. My italics. For a fuller discussion of the points I have been making see my article *Marxism: a competitor* in *The Modern Churchman*. October 1958.

whom no one could possibly accuse of being influenced by 'loaded' peace propaganda. Everyone knows, too, that there is a real danger of such a war being started by accident, by an error of judgment, and that mutual deterrence is obviously a condition that cannot continue indefinitely. The stalemate cannot last for ever.

Most people prefer not to think about it. But, as I have said already, the psychologist tells us very plainly what happens to people who push reality and fears about reality to the back of their minds. The rising generation is, I believe, much more troubled by this than many older people realize. If there is lack of trust in older folk, accusations of hypocrisy against them, and a spirit of revolt among some of the younger ones, it can only be said that some older people have deserved it . . . The very last thing we have a right to call ourselves is 'mature', and, as for being Christian in any effective sense of the word, are not the wars and revolutions of this age only too clearly the fruit of a colossal failure to establish justice and judgment in the earth—let alone charity?

We are guilty before God's poor, and especially God's 'coloured' poor. We are guilty before the next generation; and we *are* adrift. We have abandoned the beacon light of Christ for polytheism, for that is precisely what 'plural society' means when put in theological terms—the bowing down to a multitude of idols of our own manufacture,— the most popular being Venus and the Golden Calf.

Here then, from a survey of things about us, we have returned to theology; and that is as it should be. I have heard it said of Father Kelly that he would sometimes rush into the common-room and pick up the daily paper exclaiming, 'Now what's God been up to today?' That is the sort of theologian we need nowadays,—people who are so steeped in God *and* the reality of the world He made and all the people in it, 'coloured' and communist as well as white, that they can see the Living God not only in the past but in the present.

Some, if God wills, may even dare to look really far ahead, since our politicians and tycoons seem unwilling to do so. If anyone *can* look race, communism and the Bomb in the face it should be a Christian. After all did God make this world, did God so love the world, or didn't He? Has Christianity been a gigantic failure, or is it not rather that we, who call ourselves Christians, have dismally failed Christ? Redeemed, loosed from prison by Christ's death and resurrection, what have we done with our freedom? As an old Russian bishop, himself a product of tsarist times, said to me, 'You know the Soviets have done many things which we Christians should have done long ago!'

We are told to love God with our whole selves—heart, soul, mind and strength. If we are going to be any good to the world those of us who have the brains must think, and, as Pope John said, in every sphere we must have experts, people who are technically competent, and who while seeing the worth of their own trade or profession in its own right also relate it to the whole hierarchy of values and to the source of all value, God Himself.

The duty to love God with the mind must needs affect also what we call, in a more specialized sense, 'the work of the Church'. Here there are some hopeful signs. For example a great deal of consecrated thinking has gone into the work of industrial missions, the attempt to relate the Faith directly to the pattern of industry, that *by which we live* rather than to the places where men eat, sleep and bring up their families.

Then, again, there is the development of the weekly

parish meeting. Here in group-discussion (and we hope in study) Christians are learning to discover the important facts about the world we live in, and to face up to problems such as race, nationalism, communism, the Bomb, peace and disarmament. Here also they can show concern for the problems of the locality they live in. All this is essential if Christian insights are to be related to life concretely. In the pulpit general principles may be enunciated, but it is in the cut and thrust of free discussion that the principles and incentives of our religion can be 'earthed'.

There is again Inter-Church Aid (already mentioned in an earlier chapter). This in its turn can bring the separated churches into common action at parish level and so not only minister to the hungry but help towards the healing of our divisions. There are also movements like the Campaign for Nuclear Disarmament and Christian Action. Not every Christian agrees with all the particular points of C.N.D. policy, but this is the kind of thing Christians should be at. As the Bishop of Newcastle said recently, the Church ought to have that *sort* of activity to offer people—especially younger people.

But is there enough solid theological thought behind the kind of things of which we have just been speaking? Many people, even some who disagree with *Honest to God* have welcomed it as a stimulus to thought and discussion. It certainly has set people thinking. But what about? Will it get anyone asking Father Kelly's 64,000 dollar question about the *living God now,* in relation to the history being made now, in the real world, this exciting world right under our eyes?—What God sees in the forces churning it up from end to end which will affect the lives of each one of us individually?

What, for example, do we suppose God is doing about

Mr. Khrushchev? What is God *saying* to him? Could it be, 'I girded thee though thou hast not known Me?'[1] I wonder. What is God saying to us through African and Asian nationalism? If God can from 'stones raise children unto Abraham,'[2] surely He is doing something with the mighty movements for more justice in the world, and with the intense longing of man everywhere for peace? Yes; I wonder when more people are going to look for God and think about God (in a word, to theologize) as He is working out His purposes here and *now*, as well as in the past, and outside 'the usual channels' of Christian activity.

Yes, Dr Robinson! For Christ's sake let the Church look outwards, but also, for Christ's sake, let it hold up Christ, the given Image of the Invisible God, crucified, risen and to come again in glory. Let the Church hold up Christ as the beacon-light to man himself who is crucified by the greed, stupidity and pride of his fellow man. Let the Church so hold up Christ that men thirsting for justice, peace and abundant life at *all* levels may find in Him their satisfaction.

[1] Isaiah *45*.5.
[2] St. Luke *3*.8.

INDEX